ABOUT THE EDITORS

Norman R. S. Hollies is a member of the research staff of the Gillette Research Institute of Rockville, Maryland. He has been with this organization and its predecessor— Harris Research Laboratories—since 1950. As research scientist and project manager in clothing and textile research, his work focuses on fabric finishing, fabric surfaces, clothing design and comfort. Current research interests include the psychophysiology of clothing comfort sensations and the hazard analysis of textile flammability. Dr. Hollies is the author of over 60 scientific publications and patents, and is co-author with Lyman Fourt of an earlier book on a similar subject.

Ralph F. Goldman is director of the Military Ergonomics Laboratory at the U.S. Army Research Institute of Environmental Medicine in Natick, Massachusetts. He is also an adjunct associate professor at Boston University, and has been a visiting lecturer at several other universities. Among his current research interests are the environmental physiology of man, development of techniques for the assessment of thermal comfort factors in clothing, and physiologic design requirements of clothing. Dr. Goldman is the author of over 160 scientific publications in these and related areas.

Lyman Fourt
(1912-1975)

DEDICATION

This book is from many points of view a fitting and special tribute to the memory of Lyman Fourt. It was Lyman who prepared the first prospectus for the Fiber Society symposium on comfort and later contributed much to its planning and organization. The meeting, held in Washington, D.C., on November 12 and 13, 1975, provided the many excellent papers and stimulating discussion which formed the background for this book and should contribute greatly to the important and developing field of the science of clothing.

It is especially noteworthy that most of Lyman's career in research and development paralleled the growth of this field, in which he was a pioneer and major contributor. Clothing comfort research demands the resources of the physical and life sciences—chemistry, physics, mathematics and physiology among others—as well as the science and technology of fibers, yarns and fabrics. It is not surprising that Lyman Fourt, an unusually versatile scientist with competence in many of these disciplines, would find excitement and challenge in this area. Long before it became popular to advance the concept of interdisciplinary endeavor in solving the technical problems of society he was a truly interdisciplinary scientist.

It was my good fortune to be closely associated with Lyman during most of his professional career. He was a rare and uncommon human being, a man of unusual personal distinction and the highest standards. To many who knew him only slightly he appeared shy and seemed to embody the popular image of the scientist in a long white coat. If he mystified people, it was not because he was complex, but rather because his breadth of knowledge and range of interests were so much greater than those of most scientists. In fact, here was a scholar who was equally at home in the laboratory, university or textile mill.

This is a timely book. The dramatic changes in life styles, a world constantly on the move and a rising standard of living in the vast areas of the developing nations are all making new demands for comfort and efficiency in clothing. Lyman Fourt would have welcomed this challenge. He would be most pleased that his many contributions to the science of comfort and efficiency of clothing are being widely used in meeting these demands.

Milton Harris

PREFACE

The idea for a general conference on the comfort of clothing began with a phone call from Dr. Ludwig Rebenfeld, Secretary-Treasurer of the Fiber Society, early in 1974. Dr. Lyman Fourt undertook to write a prospectus of what such a conference should contain and this document, reproduced below, was sent to a wide variety of individuals to solicit interest in obtaining quality papers on these various topics.

PROSPECTUS FOR FIBER SOCIETY SYMPOSIUM ON COMFORT

This symposium aims to bring together a number of points of view relating to human comfort in the broad sense of the effectiveness and suitability of clothing to human tasks as well as to the environment. We hope that the contributors will indicate present state of knowledge and lines of fruitful development. We anticipate that the papers will fall into one of four general groups:

I. *Thermal Balance and Protection Against the Environment.* This is the classical area of the study of comfort in clothing. Advances can be expected to be found in regional distribution of temperature heat dissipation and, therefore, clothing requirements in the different regions of the body, and in the differences between the body at rest and at different levels of exercise. Thus the Pierce Foundation Laboratories have made recent contributions on the feelings of comfort with respect to the general environment for different levels of exercise and different recent histories of exercise. NASA has developed various working solutions for problems such as extra-vehicular excursions and moon walks or for the balance of men in a shirt sleeve environment in orbiting laboratories.

II. *Fiber and Fabric Properties in Relation to Comfort.* The contact of fabrics with the skin and the nature of the surface of the fabric, its hairiness or smoothness as well as the moisture wicking and moisture adsorption characteristics of the fibers, are involved in the surface contact relations. The elasticity of knit fabrics and the pressure against the skin influence the sensation and the relations to direct thermal and evaporative cooling. The art of spinning and of fabric construction and the modification of filament yarns to produce effects tending toward those of spun yarn and staple yarn fabrics are areas of sales interest and aesthetic interests in which quantitative and objective studies are needed. Means of characterizing the fabric surface from simple photography along the folded edge to more complex approaches and the correlations with comfort or with sensation in general would be appropriate subjects.

III. *Sensation.* This overlaps with the previous subject of Fiber Influences and Fabric Surface Influences on Comfort but could be approached from a more psychological point of view. The nature of perception by the contact senses of the skin and the psychophysical relations of feel or handle would be involved. Relations such as fiber diameter to the feeling of coarseness or harshness are well-known but the relations involving the new kinds of yarn and fabric texture or the effects of finishing offer opportunities for new information.

IV. *Interaction of the Clothing with the Body in Terms of Burden or Restraint of Motion and of Ventilation of the Clothing through the Effects of Body Motion.* This, like the thermal approach, can be an overall approach or it can concentrate on specific aspects of design such as the difference in warmth between trousers or skirted garments. The effect of restraint by clothing on sports performance as in football uniforms and the effect on other heavy work performance as by soldiers or firemen have been the subjects of study. Further studies in industrial and sports clothing or clothing for the Armed Services would belong in this group. Studies of improved protective gear for Law Enforcement Agencies are underway and should consider the cost of protection in terms of increased burden and restraint as well as in terms of the protection itself.

Drs. Fourt, Goldman and Hollies acting as the program committee endeavored to locate individuals who would be willing to review some aspect of each program area. As indicated in the Table of Contents of this book, seven such review papers were obtained. The written versions of these papers bring together much unpublished material from the various laboratories as well as raising a host of new issues about how comfort should be considered by students, researchers and commercial textile organizations.

Lyman Fourt eagerly pursued the preparations for this symposium. As a part-time lecturer at the University of Maryland he persuaded one of his students, Janice Shivers, to submit a paper based on her thesis which fit appropriately into one of the main topics for the symposium. Unfortunately, Lyman did not live to see the fruition of his efforts. On the first day of the symposium the speakers unanimously agreed to contribute their papers to a book in Lyman's honor. It is with considerable pleasure and pride that we present this volume as a meaningful reflection of the great respect we continue to pay to the memory of Lyman Fourt.

Ralph F. Goldman
Norman R. S. Hollies

TABLE OF CONTENTS

SECTION I

THERMAL BALANCE AND PROTECTION
AGAINST THE ENVIRONMENT

Chapter 1

THERMAL COMFORT FACTORS:
CONCEPTS AND DEFINITIONS

Ralph F. Goldman, Ph.D.

U.S. Army Research Institute of Environmental Medicine
Natick, Massachusetts 01760

The question "Are you comfortable?" evokes a spectrum of different answers depending on whether you are talking to a psychologist, physiologist, sociologist, banker, etc. In this symposium we shall address comfort only as it relates to clothing. Even here, we can evoke different answers from physiologists, physicists, psychologists and sociologists because comfort, even restricted to clothing, has a number of different aspects. There is the question of thermal comfort, which we shall address rather extensively, and the complication of how the thermal properties of clothing change with changes in the wearer's activity level; there is the aspect of the feel of clothing, its contact with the skin, irritation, slickness, which this conference will be one of the few to address; there is the question of the socially correct clothing, which we shall not address directly. However, I notice that none of you are wearing tank tops, or starched front shirts, so we have already addressed that aspect.

As a beginning, it seems appropriate to identify those thermal factors in the ambient environment which affect our comfort or discomfort in clothing. There are four such factors which must be considered in the simplest thermal environment analysis. The first of these, the air temperature (or ambient dry bulb temperature), although measured with a simple, dry thermometer, is nevertheless complicated by the need to generate a great deal of air motion over the thermometer's surface to maximize convective heat loss, should there be an increase in the indicated air temperature as the thermometer bulb is impinged by thermal radiation from lights, sunlight, radiators, etc. Such air motion is generated either by slinging the thermometer, as in a classic "sling psychrometer," or by using a motor driven fan to pull air across the thermometer bulb. The importance of the still air layer that surrounds a thermometer or any other stationary object can readily be assessed if you will hold your hand in the air; you sense an "ambient temperature." Now move your hand back and forth; the resultant change in perceived temperature does not reflect evaporation of moisture as much as it reflects the fact that your hand, like the thermometer, is surrounded by a layer of still air. This insulating air layer traps the heat delivered to the hand surface by circulation, or to the thermometer surface by radiation.

Dry bulb, or air temperature, is the controlling factor for convective heat loss and one can write a simple equation:

$$H_c = k_c \cdot A \cdot (\bar{T}_s - T_a) \tag{1}$$

where H_c = the convective heat loss,
   k_c = a coefficient for convective heat transfer (in our case a coefficient involving not only the still air layer around our body but also an expression of the thermal characteristics of the clothing worn),
   A = the surface area of the body,
   $\bar{T}_s$ = the mean weighted skin temperature of the surface of the body, and
   T_a = the dry bulb temperature we have just measured.

Clearly, we have an equation for assessing the rate at which man will lose heat by convection in any environment where air temperature is below his skin temperature if we can establish an appropriate value for k_c, *i.e.*, for the clothing plus the still air layer.

It turns out that the same equation and coefficient will also handle the case where the air temperature is higher than the skin temperature, but now, instead of a heat loss by convection, the individual suffers a heat gain. Under such conditions man has a very effective mechanism for regulating his body temperature, evaporation of sweat. Whether or not he can evaporate the sweat he will produce is a function of the next environmental parameter we must measure, the ambient vapor pressure, since water is evaporated across a vapor pressure difference and not the more familiar difference between the 100% humidity of sweat at the skin surface and the ambient relative humidity. If the air in this room were fully saturated with water vapor, *i.e.*, the ambient relative humidity was 100%, could we still evaporate any sweat produced at our skin surface? The answer, to the confusion of some of you, is yes, since sweat at our skin temperature (which would have to be about 35°C (95°F) for sweating to be initiated) would have a vapor pressure of some 42 mm Hg and the vapor pressure in this much cooler air, even at 100% relative humidity, would be substantially below that. One way of looking at this puzzle is that the sweat at the skin surface could readily evaporate into the warm, still air layer next to the skin surface, and then be carried away by convection to condense (as a fog if you will) as it moves further out into the air layer at a lower temperature, at which it is fully saturated. To determine ambient vapor pressure, we wet a cloth wick surrounding a standard, mercury in glass, thermometer. Again, we must arrange for a great deal of air motion since minimizing the extent to which any still air layer around the wet bulb thermometer can be saturated is critical; fan driven psychrometers or more sophisticated hygrometers could be used. We measure the ambient "wet bulb temperature" from which, using a standard psychrometric chart, the relative humidity of the environment, and the vapor pressure corresponding to the relative humidity at the ambient temperature, can be determined.

There is a very well established physical relationship between the convective coefficient for nonevaporative heat loss and the evaporative coefficient k_e, the Lewis relationship which establishes that $k_e = 2.2\ k_c$ (*i.e.*, $2.2°C = 1$ mm Hg). We can therefore write an equation for evaporative heat loss which closely corresponds to Equation 1 above for convective heat loss, viz:

$$H_e = k_c \cdot A \cdot 2.2\,(\bar{P}_s - P_a) \qquad (2)$$

where H_e = the evaporative heat loss,
k_c = the convective coefficient which describes the air layers around the wet bulb thermometer,
$\bar{P}_s$ = the saturated vapor pressure of water at skin temperature, and
P_a = the ambient vapor pressure.

To account for clothing in this equation we introduce a modifier for k_e, the permeability index i_m, as suggested by Woodcock. This permeability index is a perfect vapor barrier (permeability to moisture vapor transfer is zero), and would equal one if the clothed, 100% sweat-wetted man were slung by the heels at sufficient velocity so that he achieved the full evaporative potential of a ventilated wet bulb thermometer.

The third factor of the environment that must be assessed in determining thermal comfort has already been mentioned; the wind velocity (*i.e.*, air motion) since the man is not slung by the heels to maximize convection. He, therefore, obtains only that convection which is afforded him by the ambient wind speed plus whatever air motion is generated while walking. This complication, the air motion generated by the wearer while moving, clearly must be dealt with in an evaluation of clothing insulation and evaporative coefficients, and others will be presenting information on this later in the symposium. Unfortunately, assessment of air motion is quite difficult unless it is steady, directional and of sufficient intensity to move the cups or vanes of the usual instruments used to measure it. Sophisticated devices, such as a hot-wire anemometer, where the rate of heat loss from the heated wire is a measure of the air motion past the device, can be used under low levels of nondirectional air motion. However, since there is also a natural convection, *i.e.*, a chimney effect, of warm air rising, after being heated at the skin surface, and moving up along the body toward the head (as can be demonstrated by Schlieren photographic techniques), it has become general practice to simply estimate low air motions as less than 0.2 m/s (0.5 mph or 44 ft/min) although some prefer to use a value of ~ 0.1 m/s (25 ft/min); for all practical purposes the difference is negligible.

Attention will have to be paid to how clothing insulation, and permeability, are altered by wind speed as well as by air motion generated by wearer movement. The still air layer, which provides over half of the insulation that surrounds a clothed body, and also the air permeability — wind proofness — of the outer layer of the clothing is of major concern in this regard; others will also address this facet of clothing thermal characteristics in their presentations.

The fourth environmental factor which must be considered in assessing thermal comfort has also already been mentioned, the thermal radiation that is exchanged between the skin surface and the ambient radiant surround, as a function of surface temperature differences. Unlike convection, radiation can take place in a total vacuum since it is a form of electromagnetic transfer of energy. In many cases, radiant energy comes from a point source, such as the sun or a radiator, but various amounts can come from any place in the 4π-sphere which surrounds the body. The question of the mean radiant temperature of a surrounding environment is therefore generally measured with a globe thermometer. The globe thermometer, customarily painted black, although occasionally grey or flesh-colored, and sometimes even khaki for military clothing simulations, is a hollow (15.2-cm) sphere with a standard thermometer bulb in the air at its center. The sphere exchanges thermal radiation with the complete $360°$ field surrounding it and, in turn, loses a proportion of the net radiant heat load since ambient air convection carries the surface heat of the globe away. The 15.2-cm (6-in.) diameter is prescribed because such a sphere most closely mimics the ratio of convective to radiative heat transfer exchange experienced by a human body. In most of the environmental indices, for example the Effective Temperature used in the comfort range or the Wet Bulb Globe Temperature used in hotter environments, the reading of the globe thermometer is used directly. However, in estimation of heat transfer it would be more appropriate to use the actual mean radiant temperature, MRT. This is calculated from the globe temperature using the equation:

$$MRT = 1 + 2.22 \sqrt{V} \ (T_g - T_a) + T_a \qquad (3)$$

where the temperature is in $°C$ and the wind velocity (V) is in m/s.

These four factors, the dry bulb or air temperature (T_{db} or T_a), wet bulb temperature (T_{wb}) which can be converted to vapor pressure, wind velocity and globe temperature (T_g), from which mean radiant temperature can be derived, are the essential elements in determining whether or not a given environment will be comfortable. The amount of heat produced by the individual must also be considered in determining whether or not he will be comfortable in a given environment; an important characteristic in thermal comfort is whether the heat exchange allowed between the skin surface and the ambient environment by the clothing is reasonably matched to the heat production of the individual. Tabulated values for heat production exist for almost all conceivable human activities. Heat production ranges from the approximately 105 watts (90 kcal/hr) that is produced while seated at rest, to a 350-watt level which represents moderate work, up to the 700-watt level which an average individual can only sustain for about an hour before exhaustion and, finally, up to the maximum work capability of an average, fit, young man which amounts to some 1200 watts but is only sustainable for some 6 min.

Clearly, having a single clothing system which can adjust to a wide range of heat productions in a given environment is an impossibility, unless we go to microclimate controlled, air conditioned, clothing systems or to active insulating systems where the insulation is adjusted by auxiliary heat, or by forced ventilation or by opening large vents as a function of the heat production of the wearer. Such systems exist and, if we continue polluting our environment at our present rate, may be essential for all to wear for survival in the 21st century; perhaps Buck Rogers and Dr. Zarkof really knew what they were talking about in the 1940s comic strips. In the absence of such systems, it is necessary to address the appropriate units to describe clothing insulation. Just as it has proven useful to combine convective and radiative effects in calculating thermal comfort by developing an adjusted dry bulb temperature (AT_{db}) from the relationship:

$$AT_{db} = \frac{T_{db} + MRT}{2}$$

(40

(or by using the concept of operative temperature, where the radiant and air temperatures are weighted by the respective transfer coefficients for radiation and convection heat exchange) the unit which has proven useful for clothing insulation is a combined coefficient, incorporating both convective and radiative heat transfer. The unit most widely used in the United States is the clo unit. Proposed by Dr. Gagge and his colleagues at the Pierce Foundation some 30 years ago, one clo was characterized as the intrinsic insulation (*i.e.*, without the adhering exterior still air layer) of the typical business suit worn in those days. The value for 1 clo was empirically derived by consideration of the resting metabolic heat production of a standard man, one MET or 50 kcal/m^2 · hr; since about 25% of this resting heat production is lost by passive diffusion of moisture through the skin and by respiratory heat losses, 38 kcal/m^2 · hr remains to be lost through the clothing. The temperature difference across the clothing is the difference between mean-weighted skin temperature ($\overline{T}_s$) and ambient air temperature (under the assumption that the radiant temperature of the surround is the same as air temperature) so that in a comfortable room at 21°C (70°F), a clothed man with a comfortable skin temperature of 33°C (91°F) has a 12°C difference between skin and air temperatures across which this 38 kcal/m^2 · hr is transferred. Dividing the temperature difference by the heat flow (*i.e.*, 12/38) one obtains a heat transfer coefficient of 0.32°C m^2 · hr/kcal. Subsequent work indicated that approximately 0.14° of this 0.32° total was contributed by the external air layer, and 0.18° was contributed by the clothing per se. Thus, 0.18°C · m^2 · hr/kcal was accepted as the basic value for 1 clo of insulation. It is frequently more convenient to use the reciprocal of this value, 5.55 kcal/m^2 · hr · °C as the clothing insulation value (5.55 kcal/hr = 6.45 watts).

The clo value for the clothing that we customarily wear today at work, *i.e.*, light trousers and a long-sleeved shirt, is approximately 1.4 clo, including the external air layer at about 0.8 clo. This accounts for the statement that over half of the usual clothing insulation is contributed by the adhering still air layer. The highest clo value measured for a practical clothing system, other than one incorporating auxiliary heat, is the 4.3 clo of the U.S. Army arctic uniform. The bulk of such a uniform can be assessed from the physical relationship that, as measured on a heated flat plate apparatus, we obtain approximately 1.6 clo/cm (4 clo/in.) of insulation material thickness. This relationship holds for almost all conventional fabrics, whether they are made of wool, cotton or synthetic, regardless of weave or other construction characteristics. A substantially lower insulation value per unit of thickness is obtained as one goes from a flat plate to a thin cylinder such as a finger since as insulation increases there is also an increase in the surface area for heat loss. This relationship holds for the torso, as well as the finger, although the increase in surface area per unit of added insulation is not quite as dramatic. Dr. Gagge has suggested that the increase in f_{cl}, a factor assigned to increment the surface area of a nude man to account for the additional surface area when clothing is worn, amounts to approximately 15% per clo of insulation. Thus, f_{cl} for a one-clo system is 1.15.

Having introduced a number of the terms, and some of the concepts that we must deal with in considering comfort with respect to the thermal aspects of clothing, I leave it to the other participants in this symposium to flesh out, in as much detail as possible, the skeleton which I have outlined as a framework for consideration of the thermal aspects of clothing comfort.

Chapter 2

PHYSIOLOGICAL ASPECTS OF PROTECTIVE CLOTHING FOR MILITARY PERSONNEL

M. F. Haisman

Army Personnel Research Establishment
Farnborough, Hants, U.K.

The title of this paper should be qualified; in fact it will be assumed that almost any clothing system can come under the broad heading of protective. The main objective of research into military protective clothing is to help the designers, developers and procurers provide military personnel with the clothing and personal equipment most appropriate for their task. Thus, in Applied Physiology and Field Trials Division of APRE, the day-to-day work is to assess the physiological effects of the various clothing systems in terms of thermal balance, sweat loss, heart rate and energy expenditure. If such tests are carried out within the development time frame they can be of great value in providing a forecast of whether the item will meet the requirement and prove acceptable to the user, before it is released for wide scale user evaluation.

Important items may be assessed at several stages: perhaps by physical tests of the fabric; by trials in either hot or cold climatic chambers; through small scale trials at our Field Test Laboratory; through larger scale field trials in U.K. or elsewhere. Typical field trials have been carried out in desert, jungle and cold weather locations. The final stage involves monitoring world-wide troop trials before the item is accepted into service. The program is wide, ranging from various helmets to boots, load carriage equipment and digging tools. However, the following examples have been chosen from the program as the most relevant to this Symposium.

The techniques used require little explanation because they will all be familiar. It is believed that more use should be made of energy expenditure (M) measurements since M is such an important component in the heat balance equation. However, to be realistic, given the present limitation of breathing systems for collection of expired air from the subject, in many cases we have to rely on energy expenditure prediction equations such as those developed by Givoni and Goldman (1971). Nevertheless, although generally M is directly proportional to work done, it can be influenced by a variety of factors such as body weight, other anthropometric dimensions such as the size of calf or thigh muscles, body fat content, physical fitness, skill at the task, body temperature and time since the last meal, and the position of any load on the body.

Comfort is often regarded as a condition in which physiological change does not occur and it is therefore a particularly difficult area in which to obtain quantitative data. It is true that in a military context an element of discomfort may have to be accepted if the soldier is still able to perform his task. However, it seems safe to aim for the highest standard of comfort which is possible without prejudicing the operational requirements of the item. Certainly we know that, if protective items such as helmets and armored vests cause discomfort, the soldier's natural inclination is not to wear them. At least this ensures that comfort criteria are not disregarded as a luxury which has no place on the defense scene.

COLD WEATHER CLOTHING

For the first example of our work, cold weather clothing, it is appropriate to go into a little detail, because our laboratory was involved at all stages in the complete cycle from the initiation through to acceptance into service. During the last few years a new range of cold weather clothing has been developed in the U.K., by SCRDE (Stores & Clothing Research and Development Establishment) at Colchester, to replace a heavy parka with its fur-lined hood. This comprises a windproof smock, with wired hood and windproof trousers of cotton gabardine worn over a variable number of insulating smock and trouser liners of nylon-covered, quilted, polyester batting. The maximum number of liners which can be worn is three under the smock and two under the trousers. The trouser liner side seams are made with top-to-bottom zip fasteners to facilitate easy donning or removal without taking off the outer garments or boots. Underneath the liners a thick wool jersey, shirt and long thermal underwear are worn.

U.K. Chamber Trials

Initial chamber trials were carried out by Gilling and Ince (1973) at -32°C. Four permutations of liners were compared and the three smock and two trouser ensemble gave the lowest fall in mean body temperature, whereas a combination of two smock liners and one trouser liner gave at least the equivalent thermal protection to the old parka-based assembly and with a saving in weight of 2 kg.

Field Trial, Norway

The next stage involved a field trial in Norway where Worsley *et al.* (1974) undertook comparative assessments of the parka-based assembly and the new windproof smock and liner assembly using some 12 soldiers. The cold exposure consisted of a sedentary period followed by a march and a further inactive period. In all of these trials body temperatures were measured by thermistors in the rectum and at Burton's three skin sites, chest, arm and leg, and, for safety reasons, on the index finger and great toe. Unfortunately the weather in Norway can change very quickly from rain to -20° or even -30°C. Clearly it is impossible to assess the thermal protection of cold weather clothing if the climatic conditions are mild enough for the soldier to be comfortable in shirt sleeves order. On most days during the trial the air temperature was above -10°C except for 3 days when it dropped to about -20°C, and therefore the results of this field trial were inconclusive.

Another important aspect of this work is to measure energy expenditure since it is during the periods of great heat production such as when cross-country skiing that the clothing insulation must be easily reduced, and furthermore the clothing should allow sweat to evaporate freely. Amor (1973) using soldiers who were not experienced skiers has compared the energy cost of skiing, walking on snow shoes and pulling pulks. Three points emerge from this:

1. Below 1 m/s (about 2.25 mph) snowshoeing is more economical than skiing.
2. Energy is saved by carrying the load on a pulk.
3. The foot soldier in cold regions is inevitably involved in activities with a high energy cost, in this case up to 40 ml O_2/kg min or about 80% of the maximal capacity.

Chamber Trial, USARIEM

Another phase of this work was undertaken in collaboration with Goldman and Burse in the cold climatic chamber at USARIEM. The experiment compared the thermal protection of the standard U.S. Army Arctic uniform and the U.K. smock and liner assembly described earlier. The uniforms were quite different in that the U.S. was heavier by about 4 kg and had much greater bulk. The physical measurements using the copper man in Dr. Goldman's laboratory also showed the higher thermal insulation of the U.S.

ensemble. The experiment comprised 90 min sitting at rest followed immediately by 50 min work on the treadmill and then by a further 60 min of sitting at rest.

One aspect of the experiment was to compare the energy expenditure of walking at three miles per hour in the two uniforms. The hobbling effect of these multilayer clothing systems has been documented and will be referred to again later. However, we wished to investigate if the effect of these two uniforms coupled with the different types of footwear, that is,the U.S. vapor barrier boot and the U.K. mukluk, would result in different rates of energy expenditure. For the two levels of windchill used in the experiment, 1000 and 1200 kcal/m² hr, each comprising two combinations of air temperature and wind speed, there were no significant differences in energy expenditure between the uniforms during walking.

The U.K. mitt was wool/nylon with a windproof or waterproof outer layer and it had a lower insulation value than the U.S. mitt. Considering the temperature of the fingers in the highest air temperature, -6.7°C, the fingers cooled to 13°C in the U.K. mitt compared to 22°C in the heavier U.S. mitt. However, there was a very rapid warm-up during the working phase and then another fall during the post-exercise period of inactivity. In the more extreme conditions, at -30°C, the finger temperature in the U.K. mitt fell on average to 10°C, and it is fair to say that at this time some of the subjects were distinctly uncomfortable. Although subjective ratings showed some general trends viz:

1. lower (*i.e.*, cooler) ratings in lower air temperatures;
2. lower ratings for extremities;
3. U.S. to be rated warmer than U.K.

there was considerable individual variation. We found instances where for approximately the same finger temperature one subject would describe his fingers as painfully cold whereas another subject would describe his as cool.

Field Trial, Canada

The next phase was a field trial at Fort Churchill, Canada, a location considered to ensure climatic conditions at the extreme lower end of the range for which this clothing system has been designed, that is about -32°C. This trial, Honky Tonk II (Worsley and Haisman, 1975) was a collaborative one with SCRDE, with several Canadian laboratories, particularly DCIEM, Toronto, and also with Dr. Goldman's laboratory at USARIEM,Natick. In all there were some 23 investigators at one time working with 24 Royal Marine Commandoes brought in from U.K. as test subjects. During the first few days the wind chill rose to 2500 kcal/m² hr, *i.e.*, an air temperature of

-46°C and a wind speed of about 9 m/s. The first week consisted of controlled trials of various items of hand wear and foot wear, together with energy expenditure determinations in the laboratory area. For the handwear/footwear trials the subjects sat outside the laboratory until finger temperatures approached withdrawal criterion of between 10 and 5°C. They then spent 20 min walking and returned for a further period of sitting. At night sleeping bag trials were conducted in a tent pitched outside the laboratory.

During this work Gooderson compared the U.K. and the Canadian mitt using a crossover experimental design from morning to afternoon. The Canadian mitt consisted of a polyester quilted fabric inner and a leather outer with fur on the back of the hand. On one occasion the U.K. mitt gave significantly higher finger temperatures than the Canadian mitt but on three other comparisons the differences were not statistically significant. On the sleeping bag trials, Hughes compared an inexpensive and slightly lighter bag, the GS bag (modified) with the down-filled and more expensive Arctic Bag. The trials took place in an unheated tent outside the laboratory and groups of six subjects participated on two consecutive nights. The results showed a consistent and steady fall in mean body temperature of about 1.5°C during the course of the 6 hours, with very little difference in body temperatures between the two bags. On removal from the sleeping bags the soldiers responded to questions on comfort for particular areas of the body and the results supported the physiological findings in that there was little difference in the thermal comfort offered by these two different types of bag. However, they did consider the GS bag to offer inferior thermal protection for the feet and analysis of toe temperatures showed a 4°C difference in favor of the Arctic Bag.

The next phase of the trial was to go from these rather artificial circumstances of the controlled laboratory area trials to more realistic military activities. Three single-day patrols were undertaken comparing the overall thermal protection offered by three different clothing assemblies, viz the old parka assembly and the multilayer U.K. assembly described earlier, and the standard Canadian inservice assembly. The patrolling troops were intercepted and body temperatures taken during short halts. Marines are trained to move fast and some difficulty was experienced in persuading them to adopt a slower pace, so there was some degree of overheating during these first patrols until they adopted a more sensible rate of work for these severe climates. They were allowed to adjust the clothing and the number of layers of clothing for their particular notion of comfort. There was very little difference between the body temperatures for the three different assemblies. It was noted that finger temperature dropped very rapidly after stopping work, and thus the halts tended to be of rather short duration.

Another aspect of the experiment was to continue the energy expenditure determinations carried out in Norway the previous year, especially on the energy cost of snow shoeing and pulk pulling. After some initial difficulties of the respiratory equipment freezing solid, useful comparisons were made among three different types of snowshoe.

The 1-day patrols were themselves not particularly realistic because in the event of the clothing becoming sweat-soaked the subjects knew that they could dry their clothing out at night and have dry clothing for the next day. This is in marked contrast to the situation which prevails when 24 hr or more have to be spent out in the snow and when the opportunities for drying clothing are very limited. Consequently the next phase involved 48-hr patrols and compared two assemblies only. Eight men wore the parka assembly and the other eight wore the new multilayer assembly. Body temperatures were found to be quite similar over the 48 hr of activity. The only difference was during the night at which time somewhat higher skin temperatures were achieved in the new assembly. A possible explanation is that the parka was usually removed before going into the sleeping bag whereas it was quite convenient simply to remove the windproof outer layer of the new assembly and enter the sleeping bag wearing the thermal liners.

The final phases of the experiment involved a 4-day exercise during which these two assemblies were again compared, measuring body temperatures for the final 2 days of the exercise and with much the same result. Physiologically therefore, it was not possible to demonstrate any significant difference in the thermal protection offered by these two different uniforms. There remained the very difficult problem of providing sufficient protection for the hands, the feet and the face in such low temperatures. The Canadian face mask with a detachable cup served well but when thoroughly iced-up it became very uncomfortable. Some very low toe temperatures and finger temperatures were recorded in the field, a few below $5^{\circ}C$, at which point we would withdraw subjects in a cold chamber experiment. On the field trial they were not withdrawn, although medical cover was available in the event of any cold injury. Fortunately apart from the odd frost nip, particularly on the front of the neck, there were no cases that could be classified as freezing injury. Presumably the subjects were able to rewarm their hands and feet, usually by curling up of fingers, wriggling toes, sheltering inside a warm tent or by inserting the hands into pockets. Before returning to U.K. they were asked to complete a very comprehensive questionnaire on the clothing and equipment involved in the exercise, and there was an overwhelming preference for the windproof and thermal liner assembly for both the Canadian Arctic and the Norwegian type activities. Surprisingly, it was noted that very little use was made of the available two layers of thermal liners on the legs and very often they wore none. This illustrates the difficulty of adopting clothing systems which will have general acceptance among different groups of men when the comfort criteria can vary so widely. In the case of these Marines they preferred to be cold particularly on the legs and have no restriction to movement. They would prefer to carry a lighter sleeping bag, as they put it,"to travel light and freeze at night." In contrast, another group of men could well be extremely unhappy with such inadequate thermal protection in the interests of greater mobility.

ENERGY COST OF WEARING MULTILAYER CLOTHING SYSTEMS

This topic is very relevant to the evaluation of cold weather clothing. Teitlebaum and Goldman (1972) showed that energy expenditure was increased by about 16% with subjects wearing multilayer clothing compared with subjects carrying the same weight. This has been investigated in our laboratory by Amor, Vogel and Worsley (1973); M with Arctic clothing plus chemical protective clothing and respirator was found to be some 20% greater than with shorts plus weight of Arctic clothing and respirator. Tropical clothing and chemical protective clothing was in an intermediate position. The shorts plus weight results were in good agreement with predictions using the Givoni-Goldman (1971) equation for the energy expenditure of walking. At this time it is not possible to apportion the increase in energy expenditure with multiple layers into that attributable to the frictional effects, or the greater difficulty of bending the legs or to other hobbling effects. These aspects will be investigated in the future.

TROPICAL COMBAT CLOTHING

Ince et al. (1973) carried out trials to compare new tropical clothing made of polyester/cotton mixture with an OG (olive green) cellular cotton material. Physical measurements by Gilling showed that the garments were similar in respect of thermal resistance and evaporative heat transfer but, because of its open weave, the air permeability of the cellular cotton shirt (OG) was higher than that of the new polyester/cotton twill material.

Chamber trials in hot/wet and hot/dry climates were carried out utilizing 60 min of marching at 5.8 km/hr and 30 min of rest, and this whole sequence was repeated. There was no significant difference between the total body heat changes in 10 subjects dressed in the two different uniforms.

Tests in the high radiant condition, that is,about 800-1000 watt/m^2,did show a difference between the uniforms, and ear temperature was increased by about 0.3°C during 2 hr rest in the new tropical uniform. The subjects were unaware of this difference and reported that the new dress felt cooler.

However it is interesting and perhaps worrying that a number of reports were received from users that the new uniform was hotter to wear, and this seemed especially true in locations such as Hong Kong where the climate is characterized by high relative humidity coupled with fairly high levels of solar radiation.

ELECTRICALLY HEATED CLOTHING

In view of the difficulty of keeping the hands warm without restricting dexterity it is not surprising that there has been interest in providing the operators of vehicles and weapon systems with electrically heated hand wear. Streets (1974) investigated the value of the conducting polymer variety of electrically heated clothing which was claimed to be superior to the knitted wire type. In practice it has been found that the conducting polymer garments deteriorate in an unacceptably short time. In the most recent study by Streets, conducting polymer mitts were compared with knitted wire gloves (Rapier). The conducting polymer inner mitt is rated at 15 watts per mitt and the leather outer has an unheated trigger finger. The Rapier glove is knitted of insulated multistrand wire rated at 19 watts per glove and with a leather outer shell. The experiment utilized eight subjects who sat in the cold chamber at -32°C for 3 hr dressed in cold weather clothing. Slightly warmer hand temperatures were found with the conducting polymer mitt but the hand and finger temperature of the Rapier knitted glove remained at acceptable levels throughout the 3 hr. More recent studies have concentrated on the manual dexterity which can be achieved with various types of electrically heated gloves and mitts. Unfortunately until there is a breakthrough in battery development this does not help the infantryman on foot who may require electrically heated protection for the hands and feet in a static situation.

BODY ARMOR

Body armor was used extensively in Roman times, but by the end of the 16th century it had to be so heavy to protect against musket shot that it was not possible to support the weight for any length of time. In 1590 it was reported that some troops actually refused to wear it. Today vests are made up of many layers of nylon or similar material and weigh about 4 kg to give protection against fragments and low velocity missiles. Protection against the high velocity rifle bullet is usually obtained by the insertion of plates into the front and the back of the vest; in the case of the ceramic plates this may result in a total weight of about 10 kg. Clearly it is inappropriate to apply normal criteria of comfort to such a garment. However skillful the design it is still going to be heavy and inevitably it will impede movement, breathing and heat dissipation. However, in a life-threatening situation a soldier may be pleased to wear it. Our study (Haisman and Crotty, 1975) seeks to examine the effect of varying weights and designs of body armor to provide a physiological yardstick and to quantify the decrease in performance which will enable the designers to obtain the best possible compromise between protection offered and the physiological cost of this protection.

The study involves a number of phases in the laboratory, the climatic chamber and the field. One small trial at our field test laboratory involved performance on an agility course and during an 8-km (5-mi) march. These results indicate little difference in the time for nine soldiers to complete the march either in the combat uniform, the combat uniform plus 2.5 kg of armored vest or with the equivalent weight of the vest. Physiological measures of heart rate or sweat rate also showed no differences. However, the agility course scores performed both immediately before and immediately after the march did reveal a significant difference after the march with the armored vest producing the slowest times.

PREDICTION OF PHYSIOLOGICAL RESPONSES TO HOT ENVIRONMENTS

In view of the practical difficulty of fitting human factors trials into the time normally available, there is great scope for methods which allow prediction of physiological responses from a specification of the man, his activity, clothing and the environmental conditions (Givoni and Goldman, 1972). An earlier study on body armor carried out in collaboration with Goldman (Haisman and Goldman, 1974) illustrated the potential value of such methods of prediction.

The study involved eight men walking with loads of about 26 kg in a hot wet ($35°C$, 70% R.H.) and a hot dry ($49°C$, 21% R.H.) climate, and three uniform systems were compared which included a standard armored vest and a lightweight vest, both worn over a tropical fatigue uniform, and a tropical fatigue uniform without armor. All uniform systems were brought to the same weight by the addition of lead weights.

The armored uniforms were associated with higher total sweat production, a lower ratio of evaporated to total sweat, and higher rectal and mean skin temperatures compared to the no armor condition. The metabolic rate was very slightly but significantly higher in the hot wet climate and the metabolic rates themselves were only slightly higher than the predicted value using the Givoni-Goldman (1971) equation for this body weight, load and speed.

Rectal temperature was predicted using previously published equations (Givoni and Goldman, 1972) and using a "pumping coefficient" for body armor derived from a preliminary study. The agreement between the mean observed rectal temperature and that predicted for the body armor condition was found to be within $0.25^\circ C$ for the hot wet climate, and somewhat less precise, within $0.31^\circ C$ for the hot dry. It is considered that this prediction system can have practical value now although further research is required on the refinement of pumping coefficients and further validation.

In conclusion some topics from the APRE physiological work program have been reviewed, namely cold weather clothing, tropical clothing, electrically heated clothing and finally body armor. These topics all relate to the problems of comfort within protective clothing systems.

REFERENCES

Amor, A. E., J. A. Vogel and D. E. Worsley. "The Energy Cost of Wearing Multi-layer Clothing," APRE Technical Memorandum (1973).

Gilling, D. R. and N. E. Ince. "Cold Chamber Trials of Windproof Smock and Trousers with Thermal Liners Against In-service Cold Weather Clothing. Trial 1. $-32^\circ C$ Minimal Air Movement," APRE Report (1973).

Givoni, B. and R. F. Goldman. "Predicting Metabolic Energy Cost," *J. Appl. Physiol.* 30:429–433 (1971).

Givoni, B. and R. F. Goldman. "Predicting Rectal Temperature Response to Work, Environment and Clothing," *J. Appl. Physiol.* 32:812–822 (1972).

Haisman, M. F. and J. Crotty. "Problems Associated with Body Armour," APRE Advance Report No. 54 (1975).

Haisman, M. E. and R. F. Goldman. "Physiological Evaluations of Armoured Vests in Hot Wet and Hot Dry Climates," *Ergonomics* 17:1-12 (1974).

Ince, N.E., B. Cheeseman and D. R. Gilling. "A Comparative Chamber Trial of the New Tropical Combat Dress and the In-service Green Tropical Combat Clothing," APRE Report (1973).

Streets, D. E. "Cold Chamber Trial of Electrically Heated Gloves, Mitts and Insoles for Rapier Operators and AFV Crewmen," APRE Report (1974).

Teitlebaum, A. and R. F. Goldman. "Increased Energy Cost with Multiple Clothing Layers," *J. Appl. Physiol.* 32:743-744 (1972).

Worsley D., A. Amor, W. B. Hughes, N. Ince and D. Ramsay. "Physiological Trial of Cold Weather Clothing and Equipment. Exercise Honky Tonk I, Norway 1974," APRE Report (1974).

Worsley, D. and M. F. Haisman. "Exercise Honky Tonk II'" APRE Advance Report No. 51 (1975).

Chapter 3

THE USE OF AN ACOUSTIC TEST TO PREDICT FABRIC COMFORT PROPERTIES

S. M. A. Fahmy and K. Slater

Textile Science Division
University of Guelph
Guelph, Ontario, Canada

INTRODUCTION

The comfort behavior of a fabric is extremely difficult to define, but there are certain physical properties which may be measured in an attempt to predict how satisfactory a fabric will be, from the standpoint of comfort, when it is incorporated in a garment destined to be worn in a particular environmental situation. Unfortunately, the measurement of these properties can be tedious, expensive and imprecise in certain cases, so that their estimation cannot be carried out on a routine basis. For a rapid assessment of a fabric's comfort potential, it is necessary to devise some simple method of quickly providing an approximate value of each of the important physical properties. A research program has been carried out at Guelph to determine the feasibility of predicting several properties by indirect means. Full details are quoted elsewhere (Fahmy, 1975; Fahmy and Slater, 1976a), but one small aspect of the work, using a simple acoustic test to predict comfort behavior, is of some interest and is to be reported here.

COMFORT PROPERTIES AND THEIR MEASUREMENTS

In attempting to assess comfort behavior, a wide range of properties, not necessarily interdependent, must be considered. Not only the physical behavior of the cloth, but also such factors as the fit of the garment, the clothing

19

system of which it is a part and the personal idiosyncrasies of the wearer in such matters as color, style and suitability for the occasion must be taken into account. For many of these properties, of course, there is no objective method of measurement as a result of the individual variations in taste. It is possible, however, to identify certain physical properties which can be meas-ured scientifically and which are obviously relevant to the topic of comfort.

The most important examples are probably thermal resistance and air permeability. A good thermal insulator is of great value, and may even be vital to survival in extremely cold weather. In addition it may in certain circumstances be advantageous in hot weather if other factors, such as poor air or water vapor access, do not obscure the benefits gained. A fabric with high air permeability will have a more open structure, which is likely to make it cooler to wear than a less permeable one in both hot and cold conditions. The open structure will also be ineffective in combating wind chill, so that any advantage gained by good thermal resistance of the fabric in still air is lost, even in a gentle breeze, on a cold day.

The movement of water through a fabric is perhaps the most important comfort factor in all climates. In winter it is perfectly possible for water in all three of the solid, liquid and gaseous phases to be present in an outdoor garment system. Water vapor produced by perspiration at the skin can con-dense to the liquid, which subsequently freezes to ice, as the water molecules move toward the cold air at the external surface. If a fabric cannot permit sufficiently rapid disposal of water to occur, perspiration discomfort, or even a serious drain of body heat because of the diminished thermal resistance of the wet cloth and the tendency for reevaporation of the water to take place, can be experienced. This movement of water can be increased either by in-creasing water vapor permeability or by enhancing the ability of the fabric to transport liquid water to the surface. The phenomena are somewhat com-plex, but in general vapor movement is encouraged by increasing pore size whereas liquid transport is improved by reducing pore size to increase capil-lary attraction. A further complicating factor, of course, is the behavior of the fabric in heavy rain, when the undesirable movement of water toward the skin produces an unpleasant sensation of discomfort. The attempts to make a fabric waterproof, while retaining its moisture vapor permeability, have long occupied the attention of rainwear manufacturers. It is obvious, too, that moisture movement is equally important to comfort, if not more so, in hot weather.

The final physical properties of appreciable importance in a fabric's com-fort behavior are the weight and thickness of the cloth. For a given thickness, a heavier cloth is likely to contain more fiber and hence be a poorer thermal insulator, thus producing a colder garment; it also adds weight to a garment and thus may make it more tiring to wear. If weight is fixed, an increase in thickness carries with it a decrease in the fiber/air ratio of the fabric. This change may make the cloth a better thermal insulator, by increasing "dead air" space, or may make it so porous that it is ineffective against the lightest breeze. In addition, the changes brought about in water movement through the fabric can have unpredictable effects on comfort.

Measurement of all these properties is carried out by a variety of techniques, all of which have certain drawbacks. In determining weight, the mass of conditioned specimens of a known area is found and, while an accurate balance is easily obtainable, it is usually very difficult to achieve an exact estimate of the area of the fabric specimen. Thickness measurement depends on an extrapolation to zero load after a series of estimates under different compressive conditions has been carried out. There is no feasible method of checking the magnitude of the inevitable extrapolation errors. In determining thermal resistance, the rate of heat flow through a fabric is measured and is compared with the known thermal resistance of standard barriers in a calibration procedure. In addition to being somewhat tedious and requiring carefully designed equipment, the technique is susceptible to calibration error and to indeterminate heat losses, by edge effect, unless a guarded, heated flat plate is used. Air permeability is calculated by measuring the rate of air flow, or the pressure needed to maintain a given rate, through the fabric. Although equipment for reasonably rapid and inexpensive tests is available, errors of measurement arising from pressure fluctuations, the design of flow indicators and other such factors are still present.

It is in the measurement of water movement, however, that the existing methods are least satisfactory. In assessing the resistance to liquid water movement, several tests are available, measuring either resistance to flow under a given pressure difference or using subjective evaluation of water penetration through the fabric. The latter technique is extremely imprecise, while the former one is tedious and messy; there is also the additional factor of fiber swelling on wetting to be considered. Water vapor resistance determination creates even more problems. The standard technique measures the rate of diffusion from a surface, by recording weight loss over a 12-hr period, when a dish of water is covered by the fabric. Compensating factors for the presence of air layers and the changing water level must be applied, adding appreciable error of measurement to the serious disadvantage of the length of time required to carry out a test.

RATIONALIZATION FOR A NEW TECHNIQUE

The movement of air, water vapor, liquid water, heat and sound through a fabric obviously all depend to some extent on fabric structure. Molecules are impeded by contact with the fibrous barrier as they pass through it, and the movement of air, water vapor, acoustic energy or heat through a fabric takes place by a process of molecular diffusion to some extent. There are, of course, different degrees of dependence on molecular diffusion. Air or water vapor transport is primarily a diffusion phenomenon, though absorption of water by the fibers may play some part in the latter case. The passage of acoustic energy through a fabric involves an oscillation of air molecules and the extent to which this oscillation is impeded by the barrier governs the acoustic behavior of the fabric. In thermal conduction, air movement by convection within the dead air spaces will make some contribution to the process, but conduction through the fiber network and radiation across the pores will also occur and it is impossible to allocate a fixed share of the total effect to each mechanism. In liquid water penetration, molecular movement is taking place in the liquid phase, so that the problem of surface tension will be added to that of absorption by the fibers and the partial contribution of each is even less predictable. The possibility of eliminating absorption by using hydrophobic, or chemically treated, fibers as a waterproof system should not be discounted, but this has no effect on the wicking effect caused by surface tension phenomena.

Despite these reservations, however, it was felt that there are sufficient similarities between some of the transport mechanisms to make a test for correlations between them worth carrying out. As has already been stated, the work is a small part of a much wider investigation and, for this reason, it was decided to use the acoustic behavior of a fabric as the independent variable in the attempted correlations.

A rapid method for establishing an acoustic parameter for a fabric has been described elsewhere (Nute and Slater, 1973) and is capable of yielding a value for the energy loss, as a sound wave passes through a fabric, within a minute by a refinement to the technique. As the geometry of any spatial solid/gas system affects its acoustic behavior by setting up nodes, resonance or similar phenomena, it is necessary to avoid using a fixed frequency for testing sound absorption properties. This problem is overcome in traditional techniques by using a band of noise, of fixed bandwidth, followed by a manual plotting of the absorption/frequency curve. The technique is too slow for routine work, and the new procedure uses a swept-frequency signal as its noise source. A reference sweep, with no fabric in the system, is carried out to establish the initial state and is immediately followed by a second identical sweep after the fabric is in place. An "acoustic profile" of the system, displayed on a chart recorder during each sweep, is analyzed by a programmable calculator, which calculates the mean energy in each of several preselected frequency bands and assesses the percentage energy loss in each band, as a result of the presence of the fabric, immediately after the second sweep has ended.

These values are then used as abscissae and the value of the other physical property, in the attempted correlation, is used as ordinate, the graph showing the dependence of this latter property on the acoustic behavior being obtained by plotting one pair of coordinates for each fabric in turn.

RESULTS

Sixty-seven woven fabrics, representing 12 different fiber contents (including 9 blends), 11 different weaves and a variety of yarn construction factors, were used for the tests. Weight, thickness, air permeability, water vapor resistance, water resistance, thermal resistance and acoustic absorbing ability were measured for each fabric in turn, then correlations between acoustic energy loss and each of the other factors was attempted. The diagrams illustrating the correlations are shown in Figures 1 to 6, together with the regression coefficients obtained in each case.

DISCUSSION

As might have been expected, good correlation between air permeability resistance and acoustic energy loss was achieved. The relatively high regression coefficient, 0.85, indicates that the impedance of the fabric to sound energy is considerably influenced by the fabric's ability to offer a barrier to air flow, presumably because the mechanism of viscous flow resistance is predominant in effecting acoustic absorption. The promising correlation between water vapor resistance and acoustic behavior cannot at present be demonstrated conclusively, because the measurement of water vapor transmission was abandoned in view of the length of time required (approximately 14 hr) to obtain a single value. Nevertheless, the high regression coefficient (approximately 0.9) is encouraging, particularly in view of the fact that the eight tested fabrics were chosen at random without attempting to eliminate any potential sources of variability in the selection. In view of the correlation obtained for air permeability, there is no reason to suspect that the few points plotted represent a coincidental relationship, but confirmation of the high correlation must await completion of a testing program using new water vapor transmission measurement techniques described elsewhere (Fahmy and Slater, 1976b).

Liquid water resistance shows better correlation with acoustic behavior than expected, considering the fact that a waterproofing treatment had to be applied (rather than using hydrophobic fibers) because of the fiber content of the test samples. Possibly the grouping of points makes the regression coefficient misleadingly high, though a lack of sufficient variety of fabrics in test makes this somewhat difficult to ascertain.

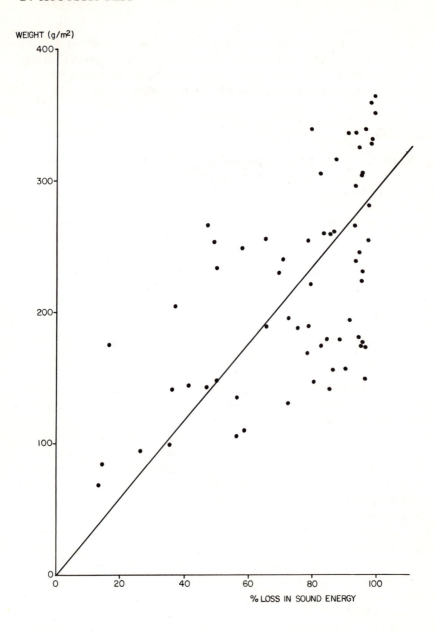

Figure 1. The correlation between fabric weight and percentage loss in sound energy, r = 0.57.

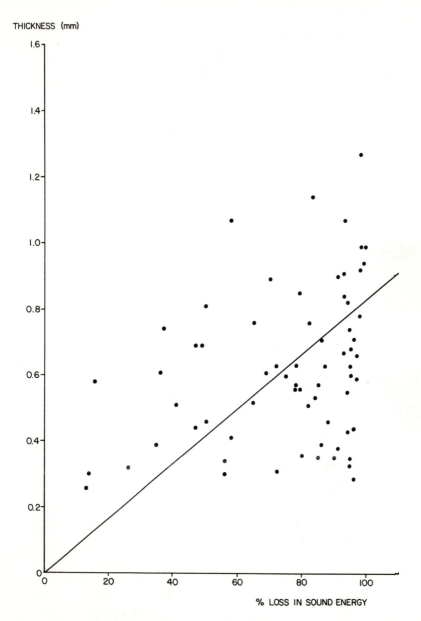

Figure 2. The correlation between fabric thickness and percentage loss in sound energy, r = 0.32.

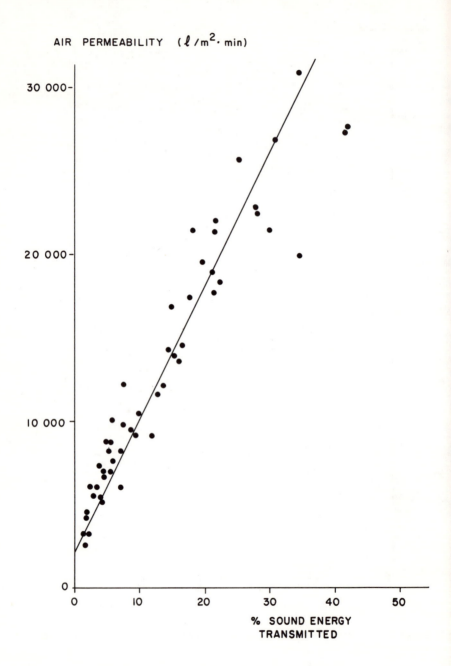

Figure 3. The correlation between air permeability and percentage loss in sound energy, r = 0.85.

MOISTURE VAPOUR TRANSMISSION RESISTANCE (cm)

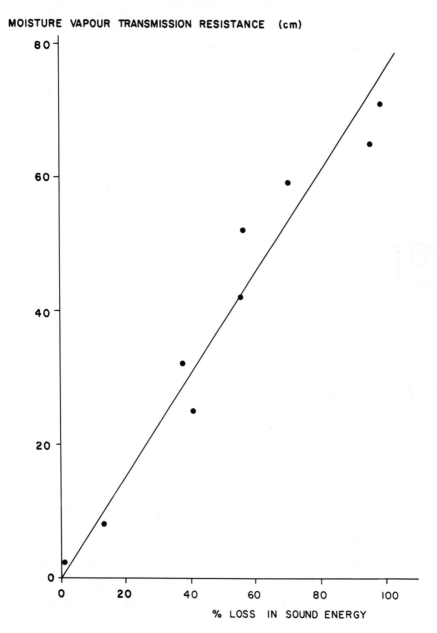

Figure 4. The correlation between moisture vapor transmission resistance and percentage loss in sound energy, r = 0.92.

LIQUID WATER IMPACT PENETRATION (g)

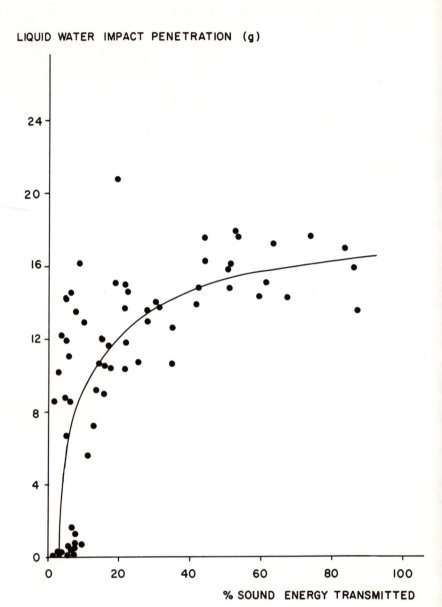

Figure 5. The correlation between liquid water impact penetration and percentage of sound energy transmitted, r = 0.64 (linear coefficient).

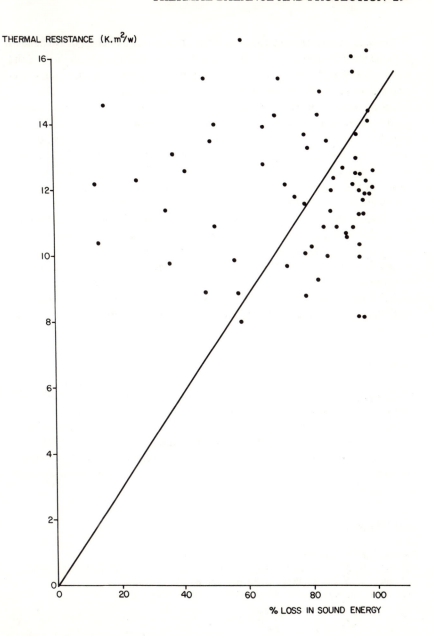

Figure 6. The correlation between thermal resistance and percentage loss in sound energy, r = 0.29.

Correlations using weight, thickness or thermal resistance as the dependent variable were low. In the first two cases, this is to be expected in view of the number of variables which can be introduced during the many fabric production steps and which influence weight or thickness. Factors such as fiber fineness, yarn count, twist or hairiness and weave count will obviously have greatly different effects on the fabric's thickness or weight and its ability to absorb sound within the interstices. In the case of thermal resistance, though, some disappointment at the low level of correlation was experienced. This test was, however, carried out at a pressure of 8 g/cm^2, a value fixed by the nature of the experimental apparatus, so that the conditions of test were somewhat different from those obtained during the acoustic measurement. This discrepancy would have to be resolved, so as to eliminate the difference in fiber/air arrangement, before the results could usefully be compared. Once this was done, some indication of the similarities or differences in the mechanisms for transferring acoustic and thermal energies through a fabric could be achieved. All three of the variables, (weight, thickness and thermal resistance) can, however, be predicted much more accurately by a different technique (Fahmy and Slater, 1976a), so this avenue of approach has not yet been explored.

CONCLUSION

A simple laboratory acoustic test, which can be completed in less than a minute, can provide reasonably accurate predictions of certain comfort properties, particularly air or water vapor permeability. In other cases, the test is sufficiently reliable to enable an approximate estimate of the particular property to be made, so that a range of fabrics can be screened, in order to reject those which are not worthy of further testing to determine the one with optimum values of the specific comfort factors involved.

REFERENCES

Fahmy, S. M. A. Phd. Thesis, University of Guelph (1975).
Fahmy, S. M. A. and K. Slater. *Proc. 23nd. Hung. Int. Text. Conf.*, Budapest **(1976a)**.
Fahmy, S. M. A. and K. Slater. *J. Textile Inst.* 67:273 (1976b).
Nute, M. E. and K. Slater. *J. Acoust. Soc. Amer.* 54:1747 (1973).

SECTION II

FIBER AND FABRIC PROPERTIES
IN RELATION TO COMFORT

Chapter 4

COMFORT FINISHING OF SYNTHETIC FABRICS

Bruce M. Latta

J.P. Stevens & Company, Inc.
Technical Center
141 Lanza Avenue
Garfield, New Jersey 07026

INTRODUCTION

Since the late 1950s, there has been enormous growth in the use of synthetic fibers. While the consumption of cotton and wool has remained at about the same level, or even declined slightly, the consumption of all synthetic fibers more than quadrupled in the period from 1960 to 1973 (*Textile Organon,* 1975). Moreover, the consumption of synthetic fibers is expected to continue to grow at a healthy rate (about 5% per year) for the foreseeable future (*Daily News Record*, 1975) (see Figure 1).

The increased use of synthetic fibers for wearing apparel in the past two decades has been a mixed blessing for the consumer. On one hand, the use of synthetic fibers has increased styling versatility, improved the ease-of-care of garments, and permitted the production of apparel with considerably extended useful lifetimes. On the other hand, the same fibers have intensified problems that were generally not severe with the natural fibers. Problems of static, pilling and snagging, soil redeposition and retention of oily soils, harshness, slickness, coolness in winter and excessive warmth in summer are frequently associated with fabrics made from synthetic textile fibers.

These complaints have not gone unheeded by fiber producers, fabric manufacturers, finishers or garment makers. Over the past decade or so, millions of dollars have been spent for research and development to produce improved textile materials.

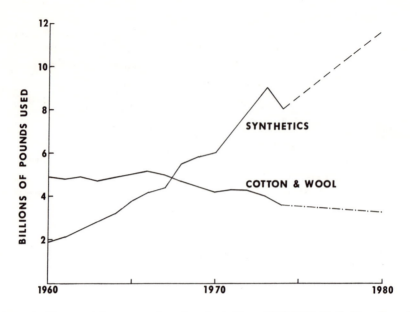

Figure 1. The growth in consumption of synthetic fibers, 1960-1980 (*Daily News Record,* 1975; *Textile Organon,* 1975).

It is generally conceded that many of the problems associated with synthetic fibers are caused by two of their inherent physical properties, namely, high tenacity and hydrophobicity. Two other properties are also considered to contribute to a lesser extent: (a) the smoothness and regularity of the fiber surfaces, a natural result of the production method employed; and (b) the lack of bulk of continuous filament yarns. Younger consumers have returned to the natural fibers for apparel in overwhelming numbers. And while older generations of consumers, who were always clothed in garments made from natural fibers in the days of their youth, have gradually accepted the synthetics in apparel, they have been vocal in their complaints that synthetic fabrics are not as comfortable as fabrics of natural fibers (Johnson, 1972).

The comments of consumers have suggested that the principal limitations of synthetics lie in six areas:

1. unnatural hand;
2. unpleasant thermal sensations;
3. clamminess of fabric in contact with the skin;
4. lack of moisture absorbency;
5. unfamiliar ("synthetic") skin contact sensations;
6. cling, lint pick-up and other static related problems.

Complete solution of these problems is within the realm of technical feasibility today. However, the coordination of many facets of textile manufacture is required to produce the most satisfactory product. Optimum comfort can be obtained with synthetic fabrics if intelligent choices are made with regard to the selection of fiber, spun or continuous filament yarn, yarn texturizing, fabric construction, finishing processes and materials, and garment design.

For example, the problem of unnatural hand can be solved by the proper choice of fiber, yarn type, texturizing, and finish (Burnthall, 1970). Thermal character and skin contact sensations are improved when yarn bulk and the randomness of fiber position are increased (Richardson *et al.*, 1957). Fabric constructions providing maximum cover for winter wear, and maximum permeability for summer wear, reduce or eliminate the undesirable thermal sensations associated with synthetics (Fourt and Hollies, 1970).

It is also possible to modify the hydrophobic properties of some synthetics sufficiently that the problems of clamminess, static, and poor moisture absorption are solved (Hollies, 1973; Moyse, 1970; Tesoro, 1968). It is to the efforts that have been made in this particular area that this paper is dedicated.

Synthetic fibers are, for the most part, hydrophobic. True, regenerated cellulose and cellulose derivatives generally retain a degree of hydrophilicity, but such fibers have not achieved the level of commercial acceptance that nylon and polyester have.

The hydrophobic character of the major synthetic fibers is derived from the nature of their polymeric components and to some extent from the methods of fiber production used. Nylon, polyester, acrylics, polyolefins and most other fibers are composed either wholly or in part of hydrocarbon chain segments. In some of the polymers, the hydrocarbon segments are separated at intervals by, or have as side chains, polar segments: the -CONH- amide linkage of nylon; the -COO- ester linkage of polyester; the -CN-cyano side group of acrylics. These polar regions would confer various amounts of hydrophilic character (ability to be solvated by water) to the polymers if they were readily accessible. Unfortunately, fibers tend to have the lowest possible surface energy when they are formed. As a consequence, the polar moieties tend to be submerged within the surface layers of synthetic fibers, and the hydrocarbon segments, which produce the lowest surface energy possible for the fiber, tend to be exposed at the surface. Surfaces of synthetic fibers thus resemble hydrocarbons in their chemical interactions, and hydrophobic character predominates, modified only to the extent that some of the polar groups must, of physical necessity, be located on the actual surface.

It is an objective of the textile finisher to overcome the limitations of synthetic fibers by use of suitable finishing procedures. Textile chemical finishing can have effects on fabric hand, thermal properties, permeability, static properties and hydrophilicity (Tesoro, 1968). Needless to say, perhaps, is that attempts to improve one or two of these properties frequently produce adverse changes in the other properties. However, it is possible to make general improvements under specific suitable conditions, without noticeably affecting any of the properties adversely.

Before proceeding to a discussion of finishing to enhance hydrophilicity, let us touch briefly upon some aspects of finishing for thermal comfort.

Thermal sensations of fabrics derive primarily from two factors, namely, the bulk thermal properties of the fabric ensemble, and the permeability of the ensemble to air and moisture. The thermal conductivity of fibers such as polyester, cotton and nylon is between 6 and 11 times as great as for an equivalent weight of air (Brandrup and Immergut, 1966; *Handbook of Chem.*, 1968; Weber *et al.*, 1959). In direct contact with the skin, fibers would tend to dissipate body heat quite rapidly. But the presence of a thin insulating air space between the skin and the fabric layer moderates the loss of body heat and moisture, and establishes a microclimate with its own temperature and humidity conditions that can be substantially different from those of the ambient environment (Fourt and Hollies, 1970).

This emphasizes the importance of aspects of finishing that control fabric porosity, hairiness, weight, etc., inasmuch as they affect the presence of the air space. Thus, fabric framing and napping can significantly alter the perceived thermal character of a fabric, and chemical finishes that change the smoothness of the fabric surface will have decided effects as well (Hollies, 1975).

Although the possibility of modifying the perception of thermal character through chemical finishing is an interesting topic, and deserves far more consideration than we can give it here, this area has received relatively little study in the textile industry to date, while hydrophilic finishing has been studied extensively.

There are several general categories of finishing processes that have been considered for the modification of hydrophobic fibers. Some of these are being utilized in the industry, with apparent commercial success. A few finishing processes are composites of several categories.

DISCUSSION

Finishing Processes

Topical Finishing Treatments

Whenever possible, it is preferred in the textile industry to modify fabric properties by means of topical finishes. This is true in part because of the relative ease with which topicals may be applied, and in part because of various economic considerations, such as the cost of capital equipment, etc.

Nearly all synthetic fabrics are subjected to some process (*e.g.*, scouring, dyeing and/or heat-setting) in which a topical finish might be applied conveniently.

The earliest attempts to impart hydrophilic properties to synthetics were based, naturally, upon topical finishes. Known structure-property relationships suggested, and it was soon demonstrated in fact, that suitable hydrophilic finishes have to possess two basic attributes (Tesoro, 1968; 1974). The finishes must have a functionality capable of strong interactions with water, with the hydrophilic functionality accessible at the air-coating interface (otherwise, the resulting surface will tend to be hydrophobic). In addition, the finishes must usually be capable of insolubilization after application to the fiber surface.

The hydrophilic character of a finish is determined by the degree of interaction of the functionality with water. Highly polar groups are capable of strong interactions with water, and those groups that can bear a formal charge can interact even more strongly. Materials with groups of these types are highly desirable as components in hydrophilic finishes. Typical groups employed in finishes include carboxylic, phosphonic and sulfonic acids and their salts, hydroxyl groups, amines, quaternary ammonium salts, and polyethers.

In general, topical finishes for hydrophilicity are of two types: fiber reactive and nonfiber reactive or additive (Tesoro, 1968). The additive finishes may be durable or nondurable as required for a particular end use. The durable nonreactive finishes are usually polymers.

One of the first polymers used as a hydrophilic finish is the condensation product of dimethyl terephthalate, ethylene glycol and polyethylene glycol (ICI, Ltd., 1967; 1969a; 1968; 1969b; Teijin, Ltd., 1974). The polyether segments interact with water, while the ethylene terephthalate segments are capable of cocrystallization with a polyester fiber surface (ICI, Ltd., 1968; Moyse, 1970). By suitable adjustment of the ethylene glycol/polyethylene glycol balance, a material is produced that is water insoluble, emulsifiable, and that forms a crystalline fiber coating when applied at high temperature. The finish is durable to multiple launderings, and confers excellent wetting properties and soil release to polyester. It does not work well on nylon or acrylics (Moyse, 1970).

Another early example of a hydrophilic polymeric finish is poly(acrylic acid) (Deering Milliken Co., 1970; duPont Co., 1963); Eastman Kodak, Co., 1964; 1966; Rohm and Haas Co., 1964; Rowland and Cirino, 1975; Yardney Int'l., 1962). This material has been incorporated with durable press formulations for a number of years. Although generally water-soluble, it can be rendered durable when copolymerized with cross-linkable monomers, if it is subjected to normal heat curing, or to an electron beam (Deering Milliken Co., 1970). The durable press resin may also form a three-dimensional matrix in which the poly(acrylic acid) becomes trapped, or with which a chemical bonding reaction can occur (Rohm & Haas Co., 1964). The polymer interacts strongly with water, forming the carboxylate salt under alkaline laundering conditions which further enhances the hydrophilic character (Rowland and Cirino, 1975). Although the polymer is durable to a number of launderings, it is subject to abrasion damage in the water-swollen state, and its effectiveness is often gradually lost over the lifetime of the treated fabric.

Polyethers are sometimes directly applied to synthetic fibers (Ciba Geigy, 1975; ICI, Ltd., 1960; Latta, 1974). They generally are used as nondurable finishes. For nondurable applications, polyethers are often structurally combined with a hydrophobic residue, such as the nonylphenoxy group, so that they function as nonionic surfactants (Barnes and Dobson, 1967; Dexter Chemical Co., 1957; Gantz, 1968). They have greater affinity for oil or for water as a function of the molecular weight of the polyether chain: molecules with low molecular weight polyethers tend to be more easily retained on the surfaces of synthetic fibers, but they confer relatively little hydrophilic character; molecules with high molecular weight polyethers confer considerable hydrophilicity, but they are not retained through even a single laundering. The nonionic surfactants may be used when fugitive hydrophilicity is desirable, *e.g.*, to provide initial moisture absorptive properties, as temporary antistats for cutting and sewing, for a special store-hand. The fugitive nonionics establish a dye concentration gradient at the fiber surface, and with prolonged storage, some dyestuffs tend to migrate into the coating. This can lead to the phenomenon of latent crocking, and with subsequent laundering, noticeable loss of color may occur (duPont Co., 1974).

A new type of nonfiber reactive finish that could have application to textiles was developed recently at Western Electric's Engineering Research Center (*Modern Plastics*, 1973). Colloidal metal oxide suspensions applied to polymeric substrates render the surface permanently wettable. The oxide colloids reportedly can be applied to any substrate, including polyolefins and Teflon*.

Fiber reactive finishes comprise the second class of topical finishes. Since these finishes are chemically bonded to fiber surfaces, they are usually permanent or at least very durable.

It is possible to graft hydrophilic monomers to most synthetic substrates using a variety of techniques. One of the most elegant methods that has received considerable recent publicity utilizes a low temperature plasma (akin to the glow of a neon light) to generate free radicals on the surface of polyester fibers (Suchecki, 1975). The radicals are relatively long-lived because

---

*Registered trademark of E. I. duPont de Nemours and Company, Inc., Wilmington, Delaware.

they are fixed on polymer backbones, and when treated fabric is passed through the vapor of a volatile monomer such as acrylic acid, grafting occurs. Although rather small quantities of monomer are grafted, the uniformity of application and accessibility of the carboxyl groups to water assures a dramatic enhancement of hydrophilicity. The plasma treatment should be useful on nylon, acrylics, polyolefins and glass in addition to polyester. The major drawback to the plasma treatment seems to be the substantial capital investment that is required. The operating costs are reported to be quite low.

Ionizing radiation from a variety of sources can be used to create grafting sites on synthetic fibers (*Encyclopedia of Polymer Science and Technology,* 1969; Katsumi and Tsugi, 1969). Some useful types of ionizing radiation are listed in Table I. Electron beam irradiation is particularly well developed, and is used in many industrial applications. The generating apparatus is shielded to protect personnel from stray radiation, and the treatment zone is maintained at nearly ambient conditions; an inert atmosphere at a slight positive pressure is frequently employed. These operating conditions contrast sharply with those required for the plasma treatment, where low pressures (*ca.* one torr) are necessary. Grafting to electron beam irradiated substrates can be carried out either in the vapor phase, or in a bath (Bobeth *et al.,* 1963; duPont Co., 1967; *Encyclopedia of Polymer Science and Technology,* 1969; Port, 1974; VEB Textilkombinat Cottbus, 1974a; 1974b; 1975a; 1975b; 1975c).

Table I. Ionizing Radiation[a]

Type	Source	Dose Rate
Soft X-Rays	Cathode Ray Tube	10^4-10^5 rad/min
Gamma Rays	Cobalt-60 Source	10^3-10^4 rad/min
Accelerated Electrons	Strontium-90 Tritium Van De Graaf Generator Vacuum Tube	to 10^6 rad/sec

[a]*Encyclopedia of Polymer Science and Technology,* 1969.

Ionizing radiation may also be used to cross-link coatings (Dowbenko *et al.,* 1974; *Encyclopedia of Polymer Science and Technology,* 1969). Ultraviolet radiation is effective when the coating is applied to a relatively smooth substrate (Celanese Corp., 1970; Inmont Corp., 1973; Mitsubishi Rayon Co., 1973; Port, 1974), but the electron beam is more suitable for most textile applications (*Encyclopedia of Polymer Science and Technology,* 1969; Mitsubishi Rayon Co., 1974), because it has better penetrating power, and is not so sensitive to opaque additives and to substrate geometry. A new development in UV lamps, from GTE Sylvania (*Mater. Energy Ind.,* 1975), may improve the outlook for UV curing in textile applications. The new GTE lamp is an iron iodide-doped mercury-discharge lamp, with an output of 300 W/in. It has much higher output in the 350-450-nm range than conventional mercury lamps, and is reported to have superior penetrating power in pigmented systems.

Radiation-initiated grafting has utility in the textile industry, but processing by these methods requires considerable investment, and is unlikely to find widespread application. Chemically initiated grafting processes would be more desirable, since they might be carried out in existing equipment. However, very few chemical grafting processes have been proposed for use on synthetic fibers because this type of initiation does not work well on relatively inert polymer surfaces (Hoshino, 1971). Recently, however, El-Rafie and coworkers (1974) reported the successful grafting of methacrylate monomer to nylon 6,6 using azobisisobutyronitrile (AIBN) initiation in alcohol-water solvent mixtures. The graft yield was profoundly improved by the presence of cupric and ferric salts. The process could be useful for grafting hydrophilic monomers to nylon, and if the mechanism of initiation proposed by the authors is correct, to polyesters and acrylics as well.

A recent patent issued to Toray Industries (1974) similarly discloses the grafting of methacrylic acid to polyamide using persulfate initiation. The efficiency of grafting was reported to be better than using an electron beam, which also tended to cause cross-linking of the polyamide. Toyobo (1974) has disclosed the grafting of unsaturated organic acids to polyester using benzoyl peroxide initiation.

Another recent development in grafting on polyester and nylon surfaces has been reported by Dobbs and co-workers (1976) at ICI. Organometallic polymerization catalysts were used to produce a polyethylene sheath around fibers. The process was shown to be applicable on a spinning threadline, with a yarn production speed of 600 m/min. The catalysts were also found to promote strong adhesion of oxide and sulfide coatings. It is possible that this system could be utilized to engraft functional vinylic monomers for hydrophilic modification of fibers. However, the process requires organic solvents and an inert atmosphere to preserve the catalyst, and thus the economic viability of the process in the textile industry is questionable.

Charge attraction between a positively charged finish and a polarizable fiber substrate can be used to provide at least semidurable hydrophilicity Gifu Seisen Co., Ltd., 1974; Rasa Industries, Ltd., 1974). Quaternary ammonium salts that are water insoluble can be applied from an emulsion to polyester, nylon or acrylics. The durability of the finish depends upon the strong attraction between the electron-rich surface and the positively charged quaternary ammonium group (Armak Co., 1972), and also upon the presence of hydrophobic groups in the molecule. The cationic nature of the finishing agent provides strong interactions with water, and enhances wettability and wicking of the fabric to an extent dependent upon the nature of the hydrophobic group. The finish also imparts substantial antistatic performance.

When ionizing radiation is used to insolubilize a hydrophilic polymer coating, some of the reaction occurs between the coating and the fiber surface (*Encyclopedia of Polymer Science and Technology*, 1969; Moyse, 1970). This provides another type of fiber-reactive finish, which we may call an intercross-linked coating. The intercross-linked finishes are quite durable because of their direct attachment to the fiber surface. Nonetheless, intercross-linked coatings that swell appreciably in water are subject to abrasion damage, and even these finishes may lose effectiveness with repeated launderings. Nearly any polymeric finish that can be applied as a nonfiber reactive topical finish can be intercross-linked using ionizing radiation. Cross-linkable monomers may be incorporated in the composition to facilitate intercross-linking when it is desired, however.

The last important type of fiber reactive topical finish is the chemically bound coating. This type is distinct from the intercross-linked finish primarily in that the bonds formed between the coating and the fiber result from chemical reactions rather than from physical processes. In order to facilitate chemical reactions, it is sometimes necessary to activate the fiber surface by some means so that reactive groups are available to the coating. For example, isocyanate-terminated molecules can be condensed with hydrolyzed polyester or with ordinary nylon to yield a durably attached finish (Bezhushvili *et al.*, 1968; duPont Co., 1960b; Perry and Savory, 1967). In the absence of reactive hydroxyl or carboxylic acid groups on the polyester surface, chemical cross-linking cannot occur, and the finish is durable only to the extent that it has selfcross-linked. The adhesion of poly(acrylic acid) latices to polyester is also increased when the fiber surface has first been hydrolyzed (Burlington Industries, 1972).

The foregoing is illustrative of the variety of topical finishing methods available to the textile industry for use in preparing hydrophilic synthetic fabrics. Although many other specific examples could be cited, including some used commercially, it would be more appropriate to describe some other important finishing procedures that offer alternatives to topical applications.

Fiber Modifications

Although synthetic fibers are resistant to chemical and physical attack, they are not impervious. Consequently, it is possible to modify fiber surfaces to a substantial degree, and to impart hydrophilic properties to the fibers themselves. This is frequently desirable, for interesting side benefits may be derived from some of the surface modification techniques.

There are several physical processes that induce surface modifications. When polymers are given prolonged exposure to plasma or high-energy radiation, partial depolymerization can occur (Byrne and Brown, 1972; *Encyclopedia of Polymer Science and Technology*, 1969; Riccobono *et al.*, 1973), concurrently with surface cross-linking. Subsequent processing can remove low molecular weight fragments and alter the fiber surface structure so that the fiber no longer has its original smooth, uniform cross section. The attack occurs at random along the fiber. Hence, the irregularities produce an appearance somewhat more like natural fibers. Capillarity in yarns containing irregular fibers tends to be greater than with the smooth, original fibers (Tennessee Eastman Co., 1973). Since porosity is increased, thermal transport and moisture vapor transport also may be significantly enhanced.

Another method for increasing the fiber surface area and irregularity involves etching (Baker, 1962; duPont Co., 1960a; Farrow *et al.*, 1962; Stuart *et al.*, 1964) with solvents, partial solvents or nonsolvents that induce crazing. The attack generally is found to occur predominantly in the less ordered regions of the fiber. As a result the crystallinity of the fiber increases with prolonged etching (Farrow *et al.*, 1962). Since the amorphous regions are randomly disposed along the fiber, the etched surface is highly irregular, more nearly approximating the appearance of a cotton fiber. The minute cracks and pits introduced weaken the fiber, and provide incipient breaking points that can help reduce pilling and snagging in fabric constructions. High temperature exposure of polyester to polyethylene glycol and its derivatives has been used to produce this effect (duPont Co., 1960a).

Crystalline polymers can be decrystallized by rapid quenching after heating to the molten state (Latta, unpublished). The properties of decrystallized polymers are usually quite different from the more normal crystalline, oriented form that fibers take. For example, decrystallized polyester has a moisture regain several times that of normal fiber, and reasonably strong bonds can be formed between decrystallized fibers by hot pressing. A decrystallized polyester surface is more wettable and provides better coating adhesion than crystalline polyester. When high energy infrared lasers became available several years ago, it became possible to decrystallize fiber surfaces by heating them rapidly to the melt by absorption of the infrared radiation, and then permitting them to air quench and preserve the decrystallized state.

A power density of 5 watt/cm^2 at 10.6 μ from a CO_2 laser is capable of melting poly(ethylene terephthalate) surfaces that are directly illuminated by the beam. The beam may be scanned with a rotating mirror, while the substrate is moved normal to the scanning direction, to provide total coverage. The configuration is shown in Figure 2. As soon as the substrate has moved past the beam, air quenching occurs.

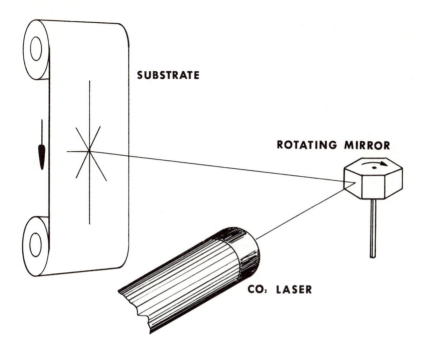

Figure 2. Configuration for laser decrystallization of film or fabric substrates.

The major limitation of decrystallized polyester is that this state is unstable; the polymer is not truly amorphous, but contains many tiny crystallites which grow over a period of several days until the surface is finally crystalline once more. This growth occurs even at temperatures well below the Tg. In the meanwhile, however, the wettability and adhesion of the decrystallized surface may be utilized advantageously. Moreover, the loss of surface orientation is permanent. Although all work to date has been done on polyester, other thermoplastic fibers might similarly be decrystallized using laser irradiation.

Another type of physical surface modification was recently disclosed by Asahi Chemical Company (1974). A suspension of abrasive particles is used in combination with alkali and ultrasound to roughen the surfaces of polyester fibers. Methods using hot, very fine silica particles in a fluidized bath have also been suggested to effectively "sand" fiber surfaces and provide irregularity.

Physical methods of surface modification have not found widespread utilization. Chemical methods have been used more generally. The oxidation of surfaces is possible for many polymers. Polyester and polypropylene materials may be treated with chromic acid or other oxidants to impart hydrophilic groups (duPont Co., 1962; FMC Corp., 1974; Kato, 1975). The treated surface is rendered considerably more hydrophilic.

The adhesion of many polymeric substrates, particularly in the packaging film industry, is enhanced by the application of a flame treatment (duPont Co., 1964; 1965; ICI, Ltd., 1958). This type of process could easily be adapted to the textile industry, where singeing operations using similar apparatus are routinely performed on spun fabrics. Greater hydrophilic character would be anticipated through the use of an oxidizing flame.

Surface hydrolysis has been described as a method to increase the hydrophilicity of polyester fabric (duPont Co., 1958; ICI, Ltd., 1951; 1952; 1964; Liljemark and Asnes, 1971; Mitsubishi Rayon Co., 1975; Namboori, 1969; Tennessee Eastman Co., 1973; Toray Industries, Inc., 1973). Through the action of a caustic solution at elevated temperatures, portions of the polyester molecules are cleaved to produce terminal hydroxyl and carboxylate groups, as depicted in Figure 3. The reaction can be accelerated by the addition of quaternary ammonium salts to the bath (ICI, Ltd., 1964). The hydrolysis reaction generally removes a considerable amount of material from the fabric, and consequently produces a softer hand (ICI, Ltd., 1951). Even if further hydrolysis were to occur in laundering, the new groups generated would be identical with those initially present, so no net change would result. As was mentioned earlier, hydrolyzed polyester provides better adhesion for a variety of topical finishes (Burlington Industries, 1972; Deering Milliken Co., 1970; duPont Co., 1960b; Eastman Kodak Co., 1966; ICI, Ltd., 1960; Toray Industries, Inc., 1973).

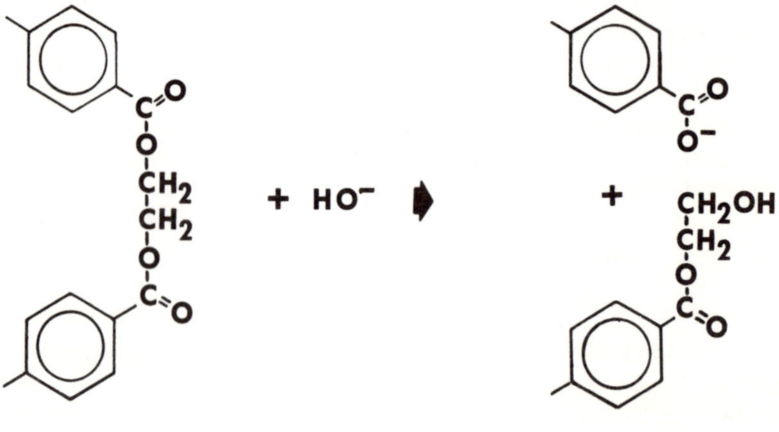

Figure 3. Caustic hydrolysis of poly(ethylene terephthalate).

In much the same manner, nylon could be hydrolyzed to produce amine and carboxylic acid terminal groups. Hydrolysis of nylon is more readily accomplished under acidic conditions (*Handbook of Industrial Textiles*, 1963), and control of the reaction might be more difficult. However, similar improvements in hydrophilic properties would be expected.

The nitrile group of acrylics is also susceptible to hydrolysis, but with the formation of undesirable color centers, which require additional processing to eliminate (Dow Chemical Co., 1964). Consequently, this method of modification is of limited value for acrylics.

Processes involving the transesterification of polyester, or transamidation of nylon have been proposed (Fiber Industries, Inc., 1968; ICI, Ltd., 1960; Yardney Int'l. Corp., 1962). Typically, a polyethylene glycol having either terminal hydroxyl or amino groups is applied to the fabric, which is then heated in the presence of a catalyst. When polyester is the substrate, some of the ethylene glycol segments are replaced by PEG. Similarly, the reaction on nylon replaces some of the surface amine segments. The surface is rendered similar chemically to the poly(ester ether) described earlier as a topical finish (Moyse, 1970). Although quite a significant improvement in hydrophilicity can be produced by transesterification reactions, problems of fabric discoloration, hand change, and the probable requirement of an afterwash must be faced. Reactions of this type are limited, of course, to condensation polymers.

There are many other organic reactions that could be employed in finishing synthetic fabrics for comfort, but many of these would require nonaqueous media or special equipment not usually found in textile finishing mills.

Let us now turn to another aspect of comfort finishing, namely, the evaluation of comfort finishes.

Wetting Behavior of Hydrophilic Textiles

The hypothesis has been advanced that the moisture transport properties of a fabric are important in determining the comfort of garments made from it (Fourt and Hollies, 1970; Harper, 1973; Hollies, 1969; Weiner, 1971). There are several physical properties pertaining to moisture transport that may be considered. These are:

1. wettability, or the rate at which liquid moisture applied to a fabric surface is adsorbed;
2. wicking, or the rate at which adsorbed moisture is dispersed over fabric volume;
3. moisture regain, or the amount of water vapor that can be absorbed by fibers;
4. moisture content, the total water held by a fabric;

5. water vapor permeability, or the rate of passage of water vapor through the construction of a fabric; and

6. drying rate, or the rate of evaporation of liquid water from a wet fabric.

Considering these properties in more detail, water vapor permeability is primarily a function of fabric thickness and porosity (Fourt and Monego 1960), and has little relationship to the hydrophilic or hydrophobic characteristics of the fibers.

Moisture regain is predominantly a bulk property of the fiber (*Handbook of Industrial Textiles*, 1963). Although finishes can be applied to fiber surfaces that increase the moisture regain of a fabric, the results are not necessarily desirable. Suppose, for example, that a 1% (on fabric weight) coating is capable of increasing the moisture regain of a fabric from about 0.4% to 2.5%. Most of the moisture is held by the surface coating, and not by the fiber; consequently, the moisture content of the coating is somewhat more than 200% of its weight. Such a coating will probably be highly swollen, subject to excessive abrasion damage, and may even impart an undesirable soggy feel to the fabric. Examples of such coatings have been prepared in our laboratory, and have been the objects of some of the grossest forms of ridicule imaginable. We have concluded that, although moisture regain may have important effects on comfort, it should be derived from the bulk fiber properties, and not through topical finishes.

Moisture content of fabrics is determined by both fiber surface and bulk properties. It depends upon the moisture regain of the fibers and upon the conditions of wear (Fourt and Hollies, 1970).

The wettability of a fabric can be assumed *a priori* to bear upon comfort. A garment that is incapable of adsorbing perspiration from moist skin will obviously cause discomfort under some wearing conditions, such as when the fabric is in direct contact with the skin in areas where a great deal of perspiration is produced.

Equally importantly, the ability of a fabric to spread adsorbed moisture over a large fabric area helps to reduce the wetness perceived (clamminess). Thermal gradients are not as sharply defined when wicking is substantial, because evaporation of the adsorbed moisture occurs over a greater area.

The drying rates of a variety of hydrophilic and hydrophobic fabrics have been studied by several investigators (Fourt et al., 1951; Steele, 1958). It has been shown that the drying rate for any fabric, regardless of hydrophilicity or fiber content, is directly proportional to the wet surface area of the fabric. The drying behavior of all fabrics is basically the same. In drying from saturation, there is an initial period during which water drains from a fabric. After the excess moisture has drained out, the drying rate becomes constant until the fabric is nearly dry (Fourt et al., 1951).

In a study conducted in our laboratory several years ago, a different condition of moisture application was used, which we feel reflects rather more closely the environment established when fabrics are worn than was used in the earlier studies. A specific quantity of water, considerably less than the fabric could hold fully saturated, was applied to the center of a test swatch. The test swatch was then hung vertically from a balance with a constant airflow at 1.5 mph through the weighing compartment; the temperature was 80°F and the relative humidity was 35%. Under this condition, hydrophilic and hydrophobic fabrics can be clearly differentiated (see Figure 4). Both types of fabric have linear initial drying curves, with significant curvilinear behavior as the samples approach total dryness. However, the hydrophilic fabrics dried much faster than the hydrophobic fabrics, because the 0.4-g water content had spread out over a much greater area of the hydrophilic swatch.

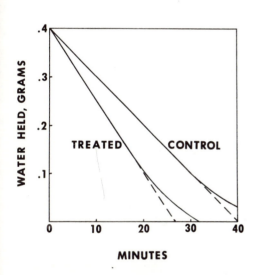

Figure 4. Drying behavior of hydrophilic (treated) and hydrophobic (control) fabrics.

In a separate test, nonhydrophilic polyester fabrics were finished by application of a rewetting surfactant at various levels, and the effect of the surfactant on drying behavior was studied. Small amounts of the rewetting agent produced substantial increases in the drying rates under the conditions of the study, as can be observed in Figure 5. However, when a much larger quantity was applied, the drying rate began to decrease. This behavior was felt to be caused by blockage of the interfiber capillaries by the surfactant residues (Hoffman, 1968).

A strong correlation was found between the drying rate and the area over which the applied moisture was able to spread. The drying rate was independent of the hydrophilicity of the sample; nonetheless, the hydrophilic

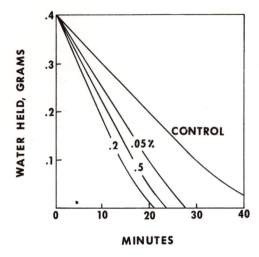

Figure 5. Drying behavior of hydrophobic fabrics finished with various amounts of anionic surfactant.

fabrics generally had large areas covered while the hydrophobic fabrics had small areas covered. Thus, hydrophilic synthetic fabrics will tend to feel dryer than similar hydrophobic fabrics because they will (a) tend to adsorb the moisture more easily, and (b) tend to disperse it over a larger fabric area from which evaporation can occur quite readily. To the extent that this factor is important as a component of the comfort of a garment, hydrophilic fabrics are more comfortable than hydrophobic fabrics.

Wear Testing of Hydrophilic Fabrics

Although specific properties related to comfort can be studied in the laboratory, only wear tests provide a practical measurement of garment comfort under actual wearing conditions.

To determine the importance of hydrophilicity in garment comfort, our laboratory conducted a wear test comparing polyester garments that differed only in their finish. Since the test was conducted in an air-conditioned office, we had anticipated that the relatively constant atmospheric conditions would negate the effects of the outside weather (Elsea and Terwillinger, 1963). However, we quickly learned that the attitudes of the wearers were profoundly affected by the external weather conditions.

Eighteen women participated in the wear test, and each was provided with two garments: one made of a standard finished polyester fabric; the other of a hydrophilic finished polyester fabric. The wear test was arranged so that about half the wearers on any given day wore hydrophilic garments, and the others wore the regularly finished garments.

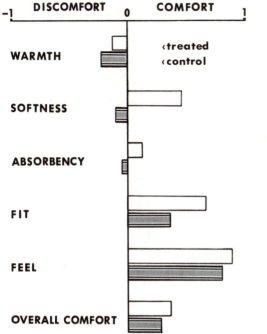

Figure 6. Wearers' judgments concerning various comfort aspects of hydrophilic and hydrophobic garments.

After 6 hr of wear each day, the wearers were asked to judge the garment with regard to warmth, hand, absorbency, feel against the skin, garment fit and general comfort. The responses varied considerably from day to day as the outside weather changed. Overall, however, the wearers tended to favor the hydrophilic garments for each of these properties. For softness, fit and absorbency, the differences in preference were more pronounced, though not statistically significant (see Figure 6).

Differences between the two types of finish were most pronounced with pantsuits, where greater skin contact was made. The other type of garment used was a long sleeved dress which made skin contact primarily on the arms and across the shoulders.

When the outside weather conditions were either very cool or very warm and humid, the difference between the finishes was insignificant. But when the temperature-humidity index (THI) was in the 75–76 range, the hydrophilic garments were reported to be more comfortable by about half the wearers. The wearers graded comfort on a scale from 1 to 5; the average comfort rating for the hydrophilic garments was greater by 0.32 units in the 75-76-THI range (see Figure 7). Consequently, though many wearers felt more comfortable in the hydrophilic garments than in the hydrophobic ones, the average rating improvement was only about 10%.

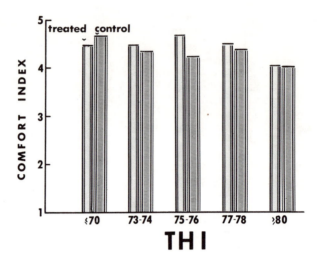

Figure 7. Wearers' judgments of overall comfort according to the temperature–humidity index (THI).

As a result of this and other wear tests, we have drawn the following conclusions:

1. The importance of hydrophilicity as a factor of comfort is related directly to the amount of skin contact made by the garment.
2. Differences in comfort between hydrophilic and hydrophobic garments are most evident under conditions of only moderate environmental stress (for example, when the THI is in the 75–76 range).
3. The presence of excessive perspiration, as from physical exercise, enhances the importance of moisture transport in garment comfort.

The ability to provide improved comfort in synthetic fabrics by finishing exists. It can, and does, provide some marketing advantage to the textile company and garment manufacturers who can offer it. There are many finishing approaches among which to choose, and they vary considerably in their capital requirements and cost of application. In general, the finishing methods that cost the least will be the most widely accepted in the textile industry.

REFERENCES

Armak Co., *Arquad Tech. Bull.* (1972).
Asahi Chem. Ind. Co., Ltd., Jap. Pat. 42,873/74, November, 1974.
Baker, W. P., Jr. *J. Polymer Sci.* 57:993-1007 (1962).
Barnes, W. V. and S. Dobson. *J. Soc. Dyers & Colorists* 83:313-320 (1967).
Bezhushvili, T. B. *et al. Khim. Volokna* 1:36-38 (1968).
Bobeth, W. A. *et al. Faserforsch. u. Textiltechnik* 24:412-417 (1963).
Brandrup, J. and E. H. Immergut. *Polymer Handbook* (New York: Interscience Publishers, 1966), pp. V1-8, V1-88.
Burlington Industries, U.S. Pat. 3,650,801, March, 1972.
Burnthall, E. V. and J. Lomartire. *Textile Chem. Colorist* 2:218-224 (1970).
Byrne, G. A. and K. C. Brown. *J. Soc. Dyers Colorists* 86:113 (1972).
Celanese Corp., Brit. Pat. 1,195,615, June, 1970.
Ciba Geigy A. G., Ger. Pat. 2,264,793, January, 1975.
Daily News Record, June 16, 1975, pp. 4,5.
Deering Milliken Co., U.S. Pat. 3,535,141, October, 1970.
Dexter Chemical Co., U.S. Pat. 2,809,159, October, 1957.
Dobbs, B. *et al. J. Polymer Sci.* (Polymer Chem. Ed.) 14:1429-1446 (1976).
Dow Chemical Co., U.S. Pat. 3,124,413, March, 1964.
Dowbenko, R. *et al. Chemtech* (September, 1974), p. 539.
duPont Co., Inc., Belg. Pat. 635,086, January, 1964.
duPont Co., Inc., Bulletin D-276 (April, 1974), p. 13.
duPont Co., Inc., Neth. Pat. 298,131, November, 1965.
duPont Co., Inc., U.S. Pat. 2,828,528, April, 1958.
duPont Co., Inc., U.S. Pat. 2,920,980, January, 1960a.
duPont Co., Inc., U.S. Pat. 2,955,954, October, 1960b.
duPont Co., Inc., U.S. Pat. 3,035,881, May, 1962.
duPont Co., Inc., U.S. Pat. 3,090,704, May, 1963.
duPont Co., Inc., U.S. Pat. 3,318,228, May, 1967.
Eastman Kodak Co., U.S. Pat. 3,152,920, October, 1964.
Eastman Kodak Co., U.S. Pat. 3,236,685, February, 1966.
El-Rafie, M. H. *et al. J. Appl. Polymer Sci.* 19:1677-1684 (1974).
Elsea, R. and R. C. Terwillinger, Jr. *Encyclopedia of Chemical Technology*, 2nd Ed. Vol. I (New York: Interscience Publishers, 1963), p. 485.
Encyclopedia of Polymer Science and Technology, Vol II (New York: Interscience Publishers, 1969), pp. 703-705, 735, 744-745, 748-749.
Farrow, G. *et al. Polymer* 3(1):17-25 (1962).
Fiber Industries, Inc., U.S. Pat. 3,400,187, September, 1968.
FMC Corp., U.S. Pat. 3,837,789, September, 1974.
Fourt, L. *et al. Textile Res. J.* 21:26-33 (1951).
Fourt, L. and N. R. S. Hollies. *Clothing: Comfort and Function* (New York: Marcel Dekker, Inc., 1970), pp. 31-41, 94-99.
Fourt, L. and C. J. Monego. "Textile Ser. Rept. No. 119," *Conf. on Mil. Appl. of Blended Fabrics*, Natick, Mass. (May, 1960).
Gantz, G. M. *Am. Dyestuff Reptr.* 57:885-892 (1968).
Gifu Seisen Co., Ltd., Jap. Pat. 125,699/74, December, 1974.
Handbook of Chemistry and Physics, 49th Ed. (Cleveland, Ohio: Chemical Rubber Co., 1968), p. E-5.

52 COMFORT FINISHING

Handbook of Chemistry and Physics, E. R. Kaswell, Ed. (New York: Wellington Sears Co., Inc., 1963), pp. 364-368, 395.

Harper, R. J. *Sources and Resources* 6(6):9 (1973).

Hoffman, J. H. *Am. Dyestuff Reptr.* 57:992-997 (1968).

Hollies, N. R. S. *Sources and Resources* 6(6):9 (1973).

Hollies, N. R. S. *Sources and Resources* 8(5):3-4 (1975).

Hollies, N. R. S. *Textile Dyer Printer* 2(10):63 (1969).

Hoshino, K. "Chemical Aftertreatment of Textiles," H. Mark, N. S. Wooding and S. M. Atlas, Eds. (New York: J. Wiley and Sons, Inc., 1971), pp. 252-258.

ICI, Ltd., Br. Pat. 652,948, May, 1951.

ICI, Ltd., Br. Pat. 788,365, January, 1958.

ICI, Ltd., Br. Pat. 850,169, September, 1960.

ICI, Ltd., Br. Pat. 1,088,984, October, 1967.

ICI, Ltd., Br. Pat. 1,155,267, June, 1969a.

ICI, Ltd., U.S. Pat. 2,590,402, March, 1952.

ICI, Ltd., U.S. Pat. 3,135,577, June, 1964.

ICI, Ltd., U.S. Pat. 3,416,952, December, 1968.

ICI, Ltd., U.S. Pat. 3,479,212, November, 1969b.

Inmont Corp., U.S. Pat. 3,713,864, January, 1973.

Johnson, R. F. Paper presented at the International Cotton Symposium, Bremen, Germany, January 27, 1972.

Kato, K. *J. Appl. Polymer Sci.* 19:1593 (1975).

Katsumi, M. and T. Tsugi. *Textile Res. J.* 39:627 (1969).

Latta, B. M. *Sources and Resources* 7(6):11 (1974).

Latta, B. M. Unpublished work.

Liljemark, N. T. and H. Asnes. *Textile Res. J.* 41:732 (1971).

Mater. Energy Ind. 2(2):23-24 (1975).

Mitsubishi Rayon Co., Jap. Pat. 77,193/73, October, 1973.

Mitsubishi Rayon Co., Jap. Pat. 16,789/74, April, 1974.

Mitsubishi Rayon Co., Jap. Pat. 20,095/75, March, 1975.

Mod. Plast. 50(12):32 (1973).

Moyse, J. A. *Textilveredlung* 5:377-385 (1970).

Namboori, C. G. G. *Textile Chem. Colorist* 1:50 (1969).

Perry, E. and J. Savory. *J. Appl. Polymer Sci.* 11(12):2473-2483 (1967).

Port, C. O. *Mod. Plast.* 51(11):55 (1974).

Rasa Industries, Ltd., Jap. Pat. 40,618/74, November, 1974.

Riccobono, P. X. *et al. Textile Chem. Colorist* 5:239-284 (1973).

Richardson, G. M. *et al. Textile Res. J.* 27:529-539 (1957).

Rohm and Haas Co., U.S. Pat. 3,125,405, March, 1964.

Rowland, S. P. and V. O. Cirino. *Textile Chem. Colorist* 7:144-148 (1975).

Steele, R. *Textile Res. J.* 28:136-144 (1958).

Stuart, H. A. *et al. Kunstoffe* 54(10):618-625 (1964).

Suchecki, S. M. *Textile Ind.* 139(3):91, 93-94 (1975).

Teijin, Ltd., U.S. Pat. 3,619,276, November, 1974.

Tennessee Eastman Co., U.S. Def. Publ. T916,001, November, 1973.

Tesoro, G. C. *J. Am. Oil Chem. Soc.* 45:351-353 (1968).

Tesoro, G. C. *Sources and Resources* 7(6):3 (1974).

Textile Org. 46(4):24 (1975).

Toray Industries, Inc., Jap. Pat. 67,590/73, September, 1973.

Toray Industries, Inc., Jap. Pat. 102,926/74, September, 1974.

Toyobo Co., Ltd., Jap. Pat. 63,761/74, June, 1974.

VEB Textilkombinat Cottbus, Fr. Pat. 2,220,546, October, 1974a.

VEB Textilkombinat Cottbus, Fr. Pat. 2,220,614, October, 1974b.

VEB Textilkombinat Cottbus, Ger. Pat. 2,422,500, February, 1975a.

VEB Textilkombinat Cottbus, Ger. Pat. 2,437,270, March, 1975b.

VEB Textilkombinat Cottbus, Br. Pat. 1,392,377, April, 1975c.

Weber, R. L. *et al. College Physics,* 3rd Ed. (New York: McGraw-Hill Book Co., Inc., 1959), pp. 213-218.

Weiner, L. I. Third Shirley International Seminar on Textiles for Comfort, Manchester, England, June 15-17, 1971.

Yardney International Corp., U.S. Pat. 3,050,418, August, 1962.

Chapter 5

INCREASED RECOVERY IN KNITTED COTTON AND COTTON BLENDS WITH COMFORT STRETCH

B. A. Kottes Andrews, G. B. Verburg,
A. B. Cooper, J. G. Frick, Jr.

Southern Regional Research Center
New Orleans, Louisiana 70179

INTRODUCTION

As twentieth century man strives for and enjoys a more agreeable and leisurely life style, he expects his garments to be attractive, comfortable and relatively free of care. Freedom from care has been achieved largely by durable press treatment of fabric made from natural fibers and by blending these fibers with synthetic fibers. Stretch, as exhibited by most knit structures, is one important aspect of comfort for certain garments, such as those worn during active sports participation or those that fit snugly. Stretch contributes to comfort by minimizing garment resistance to normal dynamic movement. The skin stretch during such movement has been measured for such body loci and movements as knee, hip, buttocks and crotch during stand to sit to deep knee bend, and elbow and back during arm raising, elbow bending and shoe tying. The skin strains ranged from 14% for the back during elbow bending, to 45% for the buttocks in bending from a standing position, to 50% for the elbow in a full bend (Kirk and Ibrahim, 1966). However, garment fit that allows slip between skin and fabric will moderate any strains translated into garment shape distortions so that the fabric strain is lower than the corresponding skin strain.

As a consumer requirement, an attractive appearance of garments is possibly more important than comfort during movement. In fabrics possessing a certain amount of stretch, attractive appearance includes a resistance to bagginess during wear or recovery from stretch in addition to freedom from wrinkling and dimensional change on laundering.

Chemical treatments with durable press-type agents combined with mechanical preshrinkage treatments such as compaction before or relaxation treatment after cure, have been used on cotton and polyester/cotton-blended knitted fabrics to reduce the dimensional changes on laundering to minimum amounts (Verburg *et al.*, 1971; 1973). Treatments to improve stability of fabrics must not decrease either resistance to bagginess or fabric recovery to an extent greater than the appearance-conscious consumer will tolerate. The recovery requirement has been estimated to be 95% of total extension (*Am. Fabrics,* 1964).

Stretch is inherent in knitted fabrics; the loose construction of any knitted fabric ensures at least a modicum of stretch, hence added comfort. Although all knitted fabrics, particularly single knits, possess inherent stretch, they do not all possess the same inherent recovery from stretch. Cotton knitted fabrics that are not given proper chemical and mechanical treatment retain an unacceptably large percentage of applied stretch, or extension, that results in garment bagginess during wear. This paper examines the unrecovered extension in both single and double circular knit fabrics of cotton and blends of cotton with up to 50% polyester, and compares the effect on this property of chemical and mechanical treatments for durable press and stability to laundering.

MATERIALS AND METHODS

Six fabrics were used, three single knit and three double knit jerseys. The single knit fabrics were knitted from 20/1 cotton and polyester yarns in a French tuck pattern with 58-66 wales per cm (23-26 wales per in.) and 61-64 courses per cm (24-25 courses per in.). Fabric weights were 166-173 g/m^2 (4.9-5.1 oz/sq yd). Fiber contents were 100, 77 and 50% combed Peeler cotton, and the remainder a high-tenacity polyester fiber of 3.2 cm (1.25 in.) staple length. These fabrics were obtained from a commercial source. The double knit fabrics were of a Swiss pique pattern, one knitted from 24/1 combed Peeler cotton and another from a 24/1 blend of 50% combed Peeler cotton and 50% high-tenacity polyester fiber of 3.2 cm (1.25 in.) staple length. These two fabrics had 66 wales per cm (26 wales per in.) and 86 courses per cm (34 courses per in.), weighed 254 g/m^2 (7.5 oz/sq yd) and were prepared in the Cotton Textile Processing Laboratory of the Center. The third Swiss pique fabric was a blend of 60% combed cotton and 40% polyester, the blend achieved by alternating courses of an intimate blend 24/1 yarn of 70% cotton and 30% polyester with courses of 150-denier texturized polyester. This fabric had 69 wales per cm (27 wales per in.) and 86 courses per cm (34 courses per in.), weighed 248 g/m^2 (7.3 oz/sq yd), and was prepared by Cotton Inc.

Aqueous solutions of dimethylol dihydroxyethyleneurea (DMDHEU), 45% solids, were obtained commercially and were used as 6% solids, based on weight of the treating bath. Emulsions of polyethylene, 33% solids, and two polyacrylates, 50% solids, also were obtained commercially. One of the polyacrylates had a glass transition temperature (Tg) of -32°C and the other a Tg of 20°C. The latter polyacrylate was reported to have elastomeric properties (Andrews and Frick, 1973). Triton X-100*, a nonionic wetting agent used as 0.1% treating bath, was a commercial product. Magnesium chloride hexahydrate, used as 1.8% treating bath, was a reagent-grade chemical. Concentrations shown in Tables are based on weight of the treating bath.

Dimensional changes in the knitted fabrics during processing or laundering were determined by measuring the change after each processing step, in the walewise (length) and coursewise (width) directions from 25 x 25 cm (10 x 10 in.) bench marks templated onto the fabrics before padding. After application of the treating bath by padding, the knitted fabrics were dried at original dimensions on pin frames at 70°C for 10 min. The sensitized fabrics were then either compacted in the walewise direction to the indicated dimensional change before curing for 3 min at 160°C at compacted dimensions, or cured for 3 min at 160°C at original dimensions, with or without a subsequent relaxation treatment that combined agitation in hot water with tumble drying at elevated temperatures. The compaction and relaxation procedures have been previously reported (Verburg et al., 1971; 1973). Dimensional changes during laundering were evaluated after five laundry cycles in both the walewise (w) and coursewise (c) directions. Laundering was in a home-type washing machine and tumble dryer according to AATCC (Technical Manual, 1973) test method 135-1973, III-B. Durable press appearance was evaluated by AATCC (Technical Manual, 1973) test method 124-1973, III-B. Unrecovered extension or length increase after five cycles of extension ranging from 15 to 50% in either the walewise or coursewise direction was determined without relaxation, and with 1 hr relaxation. The general procedure for determining unrecovered extension and breaking strength on strips 2 in. wide has been described previously (Andrews et al., 1971). Unrecovered extension was expressed as percent original dimensions.

RESULTS AND DISCUSSION
Single Jersey Fabrics

Chemical treatments that modify knitted cotton fabrics for good durable press properties and resistance to dimensional change during laundering

---

*Mention of companies or commercial products does not imply recommendation by the U.S. Department of Agriculture over others not mentioned.

usually consist of a cross-linking agent such as dimethylol dihydroxyethyleneurea, a latent acid catalyst such as magnesium chloride hexahydrate, hand
modifiers such as polyethylene or polyacrylates, and a wetting agent such as
Triton X-100. The physical properties of single jersey fabrics, of a construction suitable for shirts, blouses, or dresses, after such treatments are shown
in Table I. Laundry shrinkage and durable press ratings appeared to be more

Table I. Physical Properties of Single Jersey Fabrics Finished from
Treating Formulations Containing 6% DMDHEU.

Additive	Durable Press Rating	Laundry Shrinkage (%)		Breaking Strength (w)	
		w	c	N	(lb)
— — — — — — — — — — — — — — *100% Cotton* — — — — — — — — — — — — —					
(Untreated)	2.0	21.6	6.4	285	(64)
None	3.4	7.4	3.5	116	(26)
0.5% Polyethylene	3.4	6.7	3.3	93	(21)
3.0% Polyacrylate (Tg -32°C)	3.8	4.0	2.5	111	(25)
3.0% Polyacrylate (Tg -20°C)	4.5	3.0	2.0	107	(24)
— — — — — — — — — — — *77% Cotton-23% Polyester* — — — — — — — — — — —					
(Untreated)	2.0	18.3	1.6	280	(63)
None	3.4	7.1	3.6	142	(32)
0.5% Polyethylene	3.8	6.6	2.1	147	(33)
3.0% Polyacrylate (Tg -32°C)	3.9	4.0	1.4	142	(32)
3.0% Polyacrylate (Tg -20°C)	4.1	3.6	1.2	147	(33)
— — — — — — — — — — — *50% Cotton-50% Polyester* — — — — — — — — — — —					
(Untreated)	3.3	15.3	1.2	320	(72)
None	3.9	8.3	3.1	271	(61)
0.5% Polyethylene	3.9	7.7	2.5	280	(63)
3.0% Polyacrylate (Tg -32°C)	4.2	3.6	2.3	245	(55)
3.0% Polyacrylate (Tg -20°C)	4.2	3.7	2.3	298	(67)

a function of treatment than of blend level of the fabric. Cross-linking alone,
or with polyethylene as additive, improved both fabric appearance and
dimensional stability to laundering, but not to the extent that did inclusion
of either of the two polyacrylates. The greatest effect of increasing polyester
content is improved strength after treatment.

When mechanical treatments for preshrinkage were included with the chemical treatments, laundry shrinkage was reduced to even lower levels. The properties of single jersey fabrics obtained from the combination of chemical treatments with formulations containing 6% DMDHEU and either compaction before cure or relaxation treatment after cure are shown in Table II. With the compaction method, laundry shrinkage was reduced, but with extensive area loss during treatment; in addition, durable press rating was at least one unit lower. The combination of chemical treatments with the relaxation treatment after cure gave better stabilization to laundering, with much less loss of area during processing than did the same combination with compaction. Durable press ratings were not lowered by this method. The drawback to this combination treatment is the lack of commercial equipment for a continuous relaxation operation.

Recovery from stretch was determined by measuring unrecovered extension after tensile strain. Table III gives the unrecovered extensions, expressed as percent sample length increase, of the single jersey cotton fabrics after tensile cycling at extensions of from 15 to 50%, in each direction, measured immediately on machine relaxation and 1 hr after the extensions. This tensile cycling was used to approximate recovery of garment from shape distortion during wear. Considering skin strains reported for normal body movements as maxima that probably are not realized by the fabric during wear, it was estimated that sufficient recovery from cycling at 35% extension would produce an acceptable fabric for all garments suitable to this fabric weight. Sufficient recovery from a tensile strain of 35% original sample length was judged to be an increase of less than 10% length, measured immediately on machine relaxation (approximation of recovery during wear), and 5%, measured after 1 hr delay (approximation of recovery between wearings). Results in Table III show that the untreated jersey, as well as that treated with cross-linking agent alone or with polyethylene softener, did not meet the criterion for sufficient recovery in either direction, regardless of mechanical shrinkage induced. Substituting a polyacrylate of either Tg -32°C or Tg -20°C for the polyethylene in the cross-linking formulation did produce fabrics that met this criterion. Also, recovery from tensile deformation was not influenced by mechanical preshrinkage.

The same trends in fabric recovery occurred in the cotton/polyester fabrics. For this reason, only the results from untreated fabrics and fabrics with 6% DMDHEU and the polyacrylate of Tg -20°C are shown in Table IV for single jersey fabrics of 77% and 50% cotton blended with polyester. Unrecovered extension after tensile deformation in these fabrics closely paralleled that in the single jersey fabrics of 100% cotton. Percent length increase in the untreated fabrics blended with polyester was somewhat less at the higher test extensions, but any differences among the fabrics caused by blending

Table II. Physical Properties of DMDHEU Finished Single Jerseys Given Mechanical Preshrinkage Treatments.

Additive	Durable Press Rating		Dimensional Change (%)							
			On Treatment				On Laundering			
			w		c		w		c	
	rlx[a]	comp[b]	rlx	comp	rlx	comp	rlx	comp	rlx	comp
100% Cotton										
0.5% Polyethylene	3.6	2.3	-3.9	- 9.5	-0.9	-1.8	-2.6	-2.9	-0.3	-1.3
3.0% Polyacrylate (Tg -32°C)	3.8	2.5	-0.6	-10.0	+1.3	+1.4	-1.7	-2.3	-0.4	-1.7
3.0% Polyacrylate (Tg -20°C)	4.3	2.7	+0.5	- 9.2	+1.1	+4.0	-1.0	-0.7	-0.6	-1.0
77% Cotton-23% Polyester										
0.5% Polyethylene	3.8	2.8	-3.4	-11.0	-0.3	-5.4	-1.7	-2.6	-0.1	-0.3
3.0% Polyacrylate (Tg -32°C)	3.9	2.5	-0.6	- 8.9	+0.4	+3.2	-1.6	-1.6	-0.3	-0.3
3.0% Polyacrylate (Tg -20°C)	4.4	2.6	+0.9	- 6.9	+1.0	+2.4	-1.2	-1.5	-0.3	-0.2
50% Cotton-50% Polyester										
0.5% Polyethylene	4.2	3.3	-3.5	-11.7	-1.0	-0.7	-1.9	-3.7	-0.1	-0.9
3.0% Polyacrylate (Tg -32°C)	4.3	3.6	-0.2	- 9.3	+0.6	+2.0	-1.8	-2.0	-0.7	-1.2
3.0% Polyacrylate (Tg -20°C)	4.1	3.3	+0.5	- 8.5	+0.4	+3.8	-1.9	-2.4	-0.2	-1.1

[a] Relaxation treatment after cure.

[b] Compaction before cure.

Table III. Effect of Treatments on Percent Length Increase in 100% Cotton Single Jersey.

	Percent Length Increase After Cycling															
Preshrinkage Treatment[a]	Walewise								Coursewise							
	Measured Immed. at % Extensions of				After 1 hr Delay at % Extensions of				Measured Immed. at % Extensions of				After 1 hr Delay at % Extensions of			
	15	25	35	50	15	25	35	50	15	25	35	50	15	25	35	50
Untreated Fabric																
A	4	9	20	—	2	5	12	—	3	7	16	—	2	4	10	—
Treatment with 6% DMDHEU																
A	5	8	14	—	2	4	7	11	3	6	10	15	1	2	4	8
Treatment with 6% DMDHEU and 0.5% Polyethylene																
A	4	8	13	—	2	4	6	11	4	7	11	17	1	3	5	9
B	4	7	12	19	2	3	5	8	4	7	11	17	1	3	5	10
C	5	9	14	22	3	6	7	11	4	6	11	18	1	2	5	8
Treatment with 6% DMDHEU and 3% Polyacrylate, T_g -32°C																
A	2	4	8	13	1	2	4	7	2	3	6	10	1	2	2	4
B	2	4	8	12	1	3	4	8	3	4	7	11	1	2	3	6
C	2	4	8	14	1	2	4	6	2	3	4	10	1	1	3	4
Treatment with 6% DMDHEU and 3% Polyacrylate, T_g -20°C																
A	2	4	10	—	1	2	5	—	3	4	7	12	1	1	2	4
B	2	4	8	15	1	2	3	6	3	4	8	15	1	1	3	4
C	2	5	9	18	1	2	4	6	2	4	7	11	1	1	2	4

[a] A – no preshrinkage   B – compaction before cure   C – relaxation treatment after cure

Table IV. Effect of Treatments with a Low Tg Polyacrylate on Percent Length Increase in Single Jerseys of Cotton Blends.

	Percent Length Increase After Cycling															
	Walewise								Coursewise							
	Measured Immed. at % Extensions of				After 1 hr Delay at % Extensions of				Measured Immed. at % Extensions of				After 1 hr Delay at % Extensions of			
Treatment[a]	15	25	35	50	15	25	35	50	15	25	35	50	15	25	35	50
77% Cotton–23% Polyester																
(Untreated)	4	7	17	—	2	4	10	—	3	5	12	23	2	2	8	—
A	2	3	10	—	1	2	5	—	2	3	7	—	1	1	2	5
B	2	4	8	—	1	1	4	—	2	3	7	—	1	1	2	—
C	2	4	10	—	1	2	4	—	2	3	6	10	1	1	3	5
50% Cotton–50% Polyester																
(Untreated)	3	6	16	—	1	3	9	—	3	4	10	18	1	1	5	11
A	2	3	10	—	1	1	4	—	2	3	7	—	1	1	2	5
B	2	4	8	—	1	1	3	—	2	3	7	—	1	2	3	—
C	2	4	10	21	1	1	3	—	2	3	6	10	1	1	3	5

[a] A – Treatment with 6% DMDHEU and 3% polyacrylate (Tg -20°C); no preshrinkage.
B – Treatment with 6% DMDHEU and 3% polyacrylate (Tg -20°C); compaction before cure.
C – Treatment with 6% DMDHEU and 3% polyacrylate (Tg -20°C); relaxation treatment after cure.

disappeared on treatment. As with the 100% cotton fabrics, the influence of mechanical preshrinkage treatments was small. In fact, the recovery produced by chemical finishing of all the single jerseys with a polyacrylate additive of low Tg, in combination with a mechanical preshrinkage treatment for added laundry stability where necessary, was more than sufficient for end uses where the preferred level of stretch is 25% such as men's and women's short-sleeve shirts and women's skirts.

Double Knit Fabrics

The effectiveness of durable press treatments on knitted fabrics of a construction suitable for trousers, slacks, women's pants, or suits was tested by application to Swiss pique double knit fabrics. Physical properties of these fabrics after chemical finishing are seen in Table V. Only data from 2% polyacrylate additive in the double knit treatments is reported because there

Table V. Physical Properties of Double Knit Fabrics Finished from Treating Formulations Containing 6% DMDHEU.

Additive	Durable Press Rating	Laundry Shrinkage (%)		Breaking Strength (w)	
		w	c	N	(lb)
— — — — — — — — — — — — — 100% Cotton — — — — — — — — — — — — —
(Untreated)	2.0	22.6	4.0	580	(131)
None	3.6	6.2	0.1	218	(49)
0.5% Polyethylene	3.7	6.2	1.0	218	(49)
2.0% Polyacrylate (Tg -20°C)	3.9	4.6	-0.6	209	(47)
— — — — — — — — — — 50% Cotton–50% Polyester — — — — — — — — — —
(Untreated)	2.7	17.4	0.4	720	(162)
None	4.0	6.9	1.0	550	(124)
0.5% Polyethylene	4.3	6.8	0.2	575	(129)
2.0% Polyacrylate (Tg -20°C)	4.2	6.3	-0.5	650	(146)
— — — — — — — — — — 60% Cotton–40% Polyester[a] — — — — — — — — — —
(Untreated)	3.0	16.4	14.0	375	(84)
0.5% Polyethylene	4.5	4.6	4.9	255	(57)
2.0% Polyacrylate (Tg -20°C)	3.7	2.8	2.8	275	(62)

[a]Blended by alternating feeds of 70% cotton/30% polyester with feeds of texturized filament polyester yarn.

was no improvement in properties from use of 3%, the concentration found optimum for single knits. The properties were changed by chemical finishing in the same direction as those in the treated single jerseys listed in Table I; that is, appearance and dimensional stability were increased and strength was reduced. With the exception of the blend fabric containing filament polyester, the polyacrylate treatments were not quite as effective in reducing shrinkage in the high shrinkage (walewise) direction in the double as in the single knits. However, when area shrinkage was considered, this difference disappeared. Table VI shows the effect on double knit fabrics of chemical treatments in combination with the mechanical preshrinkage treatments. Durable press ratings of the double knits were not lowered by any of the combination treatments to the extent that they were in the single jerseys by the chemical treatments combined with compaction. Appearance of the double knit samples that were compacted, however, was poorer than the appearance of those given relaxation treatments after cure. The area loss to the manufacturer during processing of the double knit fabrics that had been compacted was greater than that with fabrics given relaxation treatments. The differences between the processes were not as great in the double knit fabrics, however, as in the single jerseys listed in Table II. Two factors contribute to this. With the double knit fabrics, there was greater loss of area from the relaxation treatments than with the single jerseys. Secondly, the area loss due to compaction was similar for both constructions. These factors also combined to produce greater resistance to laundry shrinkage in the double knits than in the single jerseys from both mechanical preshrinkage treatments. Any differences due to fiber content or synthetic fiber form were negligible.

Recovery from tensile deformation in the double knit fabrics of 100% cotton is shown in Table VII. Unrecovered extension of the untreated double knit fabrics was greater than in untreated single jerseys (Table III), possibly because of the more restricted structure. As was the case with single jerseys, mechanical treatments did not appear to influence recovery in the treated fabrics. Chemical treatments decreased unrecovered extension, but length increases of less than 10% were not immediately obtained after extensions greater than 25%. Inclusion of polyethylene as additive to the chemical treatment, however, produced a greater increase in recovery in the double than in the single knits. Thus, unrecovered extensions from similar extensions were equivalent in both structures. The polyacrylate of Tg -20°C did not increase recovery in the double knit fabrics to the same level as in single jerseys at equivalent extensions, although the actual improvement was greater. The lower polyacrylate concentration in the double knit treatments was not a contributing factor. Experimentally, it was shown that recoveries in the double knit fabrics treated with either 2 or 3% polyacrylate formulations were equivalent from equivalent extensions.

Unrecovered extensions in the double knit fabrics containing polyester are shown in Table VIII. The untreated double knit fabric containing polyester solely as staple recovered from tensile deformation as did the single jersey containing 50% polyester staple (Table IV), and to a greater extent than the

Table VI. Physical Properties of DMDHEU Finished Double Knit Fabrics Given Mechanical Preshrinkage Treatments.

Additive	Durable Press Rating		Dimensional Change (%)							
			On Treatment				On Laundering			
			w		c		w		c	
	rlx[a]	comp[b]	rlx	comp	rlx	comp	rlx	comp	rlx	comp
100% Cotton										
None	3.7	3.5	-7.7	-12.2	+0.7	+4.8	-1.0	-1.7	+0.1	+0.2
0.5% Polyethylene	3.8	3.5	-6.5	-12.9	-1.5	+2.7	-0.8	-1.2	+0.3	+1.2
2.0% Polyacrylate (Tg -20°C)	3.7	3.3	-4.2	-11.0	+1.9	+4.8	-1.0	-0.7	+0.3	+1.0
50% Cotton–50% Polyester										
None	3.8	3.9	-7.7	-12.3	-2.3	+3.2	-1.4	-2.6	-1.0	+0.1
0.5% Polyethylene	4.1	3.7	-7.9	-13.3	-0.5	+2.2	-1.1	-2.4	0.0	+0.7
2.0% Polyacrylate (Tg -20°C)	4.0	3.5	-6.3	-12.6	+0.5	+2.1	-1.2	-1.9	-0.4	+0.7
60% Cotton–40% Polyester[c]										
0.5% Polyethylene	4.5	--	-3.9	--	-4.2	--	-0.7	--	-0.7	--

[a] Relaxation treatment after cure.
[b] Compaction before cure.
[c] Blended by alternating feeds of 70% cotton/30% polyester yarn with feeds of textured filament polyester yarn.

Table VII. Effect of Treatments on Percent Length Increase in 100% Cotton Double Knit Fabrics.

Preshrinkage Treatment[a]	Walewise								Coursewise							
	Measured Immed. at % Extensions of				After 1 hr Delay at % Extensions of				Measured Immed. at % Extensions of				After 1 hr Delay at % Extensions of			
	15	25	35	50	15	25	35	50	15	25	35	50	15	25	35	50
Untreated Fabric																
A	7	14	26	45	3	8	16	34	4	8	15	25	2	3	7	16
Treatment with 6% DMDHEU																
A	6	9	19	—	3	5	9	16	5	8	14	22	2	3	5	12
B	6	10	17	—	2	6	13	—	5	9	15	22	2	4	8	14
C	6	11	19	—	2	5	10	—	5	8	13	20	2	3	6	11
Treatment with 6% DMDHEU and 0.5% Polyethylene																
A	5	8	13	20	2	3	6	13	4	6	10	15	1	2	4	8
B	5	7	13	16	1	3	6	—	5	7	12	17	2	3	6	10
C	5	8	14	22	1	2	6	14	4	6	10	15	1	2	4	8
Treatment with 6% DMDHEU and 2.0% Polyacrylate (Tg-20°C)																
A	4	6	12	—	1	2	4	10	2	5	6	11	1	2	3	5
B	4	6	12	20	1	2	6	—	3	5	9	15	1	2	4	8
C	4	6	12	—	1	2	6	—	3	4	7	11	1	1	3	6

[a] A – no preshrinkage   B – compaction before cure   C – relaxation treatment after cure

Table VIII. Effect of DMDHEU Treatments with Additives on Percent Length Increase in Double Knit Blends.

	Percent Length Increase After Cycling															
	Walewise								Coursewise							
	Measured Immed. at % Extensions of				After 1 hr Delay at % Extensions of				Measured Immed. at % Extensions of				After 1 hr Delay at % Extensions of			
Preshrinkage Treatment[a] and Additive	15	25	35	50	15	25	35	50	15	25	35	50	15	25	35	50
50% Cotton–50% Polyester																
(Untreated)	2	7	18	36	1	2	9	22	4	6	10	24	2	3	4	8
0.5% Polyethylene																
A	3	6	11	19	2	3	6	10	4	6	9	11	1	2	3	5
B	4	6	11	14	1	2	4	8	4	6	9	12	1	2	4	6
C	3	7	12	21	1	3	6	10	3	5	8	12	1	2	4	6
2.0% Polyacrylate (Tg-20°C)																
A	4	6	11	21	1	2	4	8	2	4	6	10	1	1	3	5
B	3	6	10	18	1	2	4	9	3	4	7	10	1	2	3	5
C	3	6	11	21	1	2	4	9	3	4	6	9	1	1	3	5
60% Cotton–40% Polyester[b]																
(Untreated)	3	6	11	20	1	2	5	12	3	5	9	15	1	2	4	8
0.5% Polyethylene																
A	2	4	7	12	1	1	2	5	2	4	6	8	1	1	2	3
2.0% Polyacrylate (Tg-20°C)																
A	1	3	7	14	0	1	3	5	2	3	5	8	1	1	2	4

[a] A – no preshrinkage   B – compacted before cure   C – relaxation treatment after cure
[b] Blended by alternating feeds of 70% cotton/30% polyester with feeds of texturized filament polyester yarn.

double knit of 100% cotton (Table VII). Treatments of the double knit fabric containing polyester solely as staple decreased unrecovered extension after equivalent extensions to levels in the double knits of 100% cotton, indicating that treatment was less effective in the fabrics containing polyester.

The greatest contribution made to recovery by blending with polyester was seen with the double knit blend that contained part of the polyester as texturized filament. In the treated double knit fabrics of 100% cotton, as well as of cotton-polyester with the polyester solely as staple, there was only marginal recovery from the 30% stretch encountered in garments suitable to this fabric construction. In the fabric containing filament polyester, however, even the untreated fabric recovered from extensions to levels only possible after chemical treatment in the other fabrics studied, regardless of structure or blend level. Treatment with either the polyethylene additive or the polyacrylate additive of Tg -20°C further decreased unrecovered extension in the fabric containing filament polyester, and unrecovered extension after treatment was even less than that in single jerseys.

Another contribution made by blending to the double knits, but not to the single jerseys, was increased elongation before break. These fabrics could be stretched to 50% length without breaking, whereas the others could not. (Greater than breaking elongation is indicated by dashes in Tables III, IV and VII.)

SUMMARY AND CONCLUSIONS

In knitted fabrics of 100% cotton, or cotton blended with up to 50% polyester, that were treated for improvement in dimensional stability and durable press properties, recovery from tensile deformation varied with fabric structure, fiber form and finishing treatment. Cross-linking to durable press levels decreased unrecovered extension, both in fabrics of shirting weight and construction and of suiting weight and construction, but not to an extent judged acceptable for garment recovery from shape distortion during active wear. Addition of polyethylene to the cross-link finish did not decrease unrecovered extension to acceptable levels in the fabrics knitted from yarns of staple fiber. However, polyacrylate additives of low glass transition temperatures further improved recovery in all the lighter fabrics to an acceptable level of unrecovered extension after 35% extension, that is, an increase in sample length of less than 10%, measured immediately on machine relaxation. These additives produced greater than minimum acceptable levels of recovery from the 25% strains encountered in garment end uses such as skirts and men's and women's shirts, along with good durable press properties. In the fabrics of heavier weight and of constructions suitable for slacks, skirts, or suits, recovery produced by chemical additives to finishing was not enough.

Inclusion of polyester as texturized filament in the fabric construction was necessary to approach acceptable recovery levels from the higher stretch required for garment end uses suitable to this heavier, more restricted fabric. Any advantage contributed by polyester as staple in fabrics of both weights was overshadowed by the effects of chemical finishing in the treated fabric.

Adjuncts to finishing knitted fabrics, such as induced preshrinkage treatments, did not appear to adversely affect recovery from shape distortion. Their inclusion or omission from finishing of knitted fabrics containing cotton would depend on other factors, such as aesthetics, effect on fabric appearance; economics, loss of fabric area to the manufacturer during processing; pragmatics, commercial availability of the process; and effectiveness, minimization of laundry shrinkage.

ACKNOWLEDGMENT

The authors thank Messrs. Woodrow Carter, James Franklin and Milton J. Hoffman of the Pilot Plant Process group of the Center for assistance in compacting the fabrics.

REFERENCES

Am. Fabrics 63:66-67, "How Much Stretch . . . and Where," (Winter-Spring, 1964).

American Association of Textile Chemists and Colorists. *AATCC Technical Manual* 49 (1973).

Andrews, B. A. K. and J. G. Frick, Jr. "The Role of Glass-Transition Temperature of Polymeric Additives in Durable-Press Finishing of Knitted Cotton," *Textile Res. J.* 43:19-23 (1973).

Andrews, B. A. K., W. F. McSherry, J. G. Frick, Jr. and A. B. Cooper. "Recovery from Tensile Strain in Knitted Cotton Fabric after Cross-Linking," *Textile Res. J.* 41:387-391 (1971).

Kirk, W., Jr. and S. M. Ibrahim. "Fundamental Relationship of Fabric Extensibility to Anthropometric Requirements and Garment Performance," *Textile Res. J.* 36:36-47 (1966).

Verburg, G. B., J. G. Frick, Jr. and J. D. Reid. "Induced Shrinkage in Durable-Press Knitted Fabrics," *The Knitter* 35(11):25-27, 34 (1971).

Verburg, G. B., J. G. Frick, Jr. and J. D. Reid. "Methods of Controlling Laundry Shrinkage in Cotton and Cotton-Blend Knitted Fabrics," *Knit Shrinkage: Cause, Effect and Control, AATCC Symposium, Book of Papers* (1973), pp. 77-82.

Chapter 6

PARTIAL ANALYSIS OF COMFORT'S GESTALT

G. J. Pontrelli

E   E. I. duPont de Nemours & Co., Inc.
Textile Fibers Department
Orlon® Technical Division
Wilmington, Delaware 19898

BACKGROUND

As a fiber producer, one of our key objectives is to understand the many facets of comfort and, thereby, assist the textile industry to develop yarns, fabrics and garments which provide consumers with maximum comfort without sacrificing other important end-use requirements such as durability, styling versatility and ease of care at a reasonable cost. Each of us has his or her own definition and concept of comfort; *e.g.*, we speak about comfortable fibers such as cotton, comfortable fabrics such as knits and comfortable garments such as jeans, giving reasons such as hydrophilicity, stretch and style to justify our preference. However, recent duPont-sponsored studies on consumer attitudes toward comfort show rather conclusively that comfort is a subjective response resulting from many other stimuli; it is not a cause, it is a conclusion! That is, a given item of clothing, which may be considered to be comfortable on one occasion, may be totally unacceptable on some other occasion, even if something seemingly totally irrelevant, such as style or color, is changed.

CONCEPT OF COMFORT

To study and understand the various stimuli which result in comfort (or discomfort) we have developed "Comfort's Gestalt" as shown in Figure l. Listed are key parameters that cause a person to feel comfort or discomfort.

71

Figure 1. Comfort's Gestalt

These variables can be grouped under three separate categories:

1. The first combines the physical variables of environment, transport properties, level of activity and the garment (Fourt and Hollies, 1970).
2. The second combines psycho-physiological parameters such as state of being, end-use and occasion of wear, tactile aesthetics, etc. (Flugel, 1950; Kemp, 1971).
3. The last category is a filter, which I call the stored modifiers, consisting of elements of all our past experiences, expectations and fantasies.

By definition, the word gestalt implies that the comfort or discomfort response depends upon the interactions between these physical, physiological and psychological stimuli and the stored modifiers of each person, both conscious and subconscious. Note that style is included under psychological stimuli because of its importance to a person's comfort response. Thus, it is apparent that to simply ask a person which garment or garments he finds comfortable may not yield meaningful results because the garment has no inherent comfort property and is only one of many factors which cause a person to respond positively or negatively.

Thus, when we examine Comfort's Gestalt, one can readily conclude, for example, that there are no comfortable garments, fabrics, yarns or fibers. However, we all know that there can be a favorable comfort response when the garment is properly tailored, the fabric satisfies garment requirements, the environment does not cause undue stress and, finally, the subject has a positive emotional state.

OBJECTIVE

My objective in this chapter is to discuss two aspects of Comfort's Gestalt, each of which is a separate partial analysis. The first will be a detailed analysis of one of the physical factors—moisture transport in athletic socks as a function of fiber type. The second aspect deals with tactile aesthetics as a psychological stimulus. For this subject, I have chosen to discuss women's dresses, men's slacks and T-shirts. To be consistent with this partial analysis approach, I will avoid using the word comfort. All subjective responses in this study are answers to the questions, "Which garment do you prefer?" and "Why?" Each of you can draw your own conclusion as to whether the responses indicate comfort or discomfort.

THE EFFECT OF MOISTURE
TRANSPORT IN ATHLETIC SOCKS

Based on articles (Wilson, 1975) and discussions (Pontrelli, 1975) with athletic directors and team physicians from professional and college teams, natural fibers are almost universally recommended versus synthetics because they absorb more sweat and, therefore, it is generally concluded that they keep feet drier. The latter condition is important to athletes because it minimizes blistering by reducing foot-to-sock/sneaker friction. However, one must ask why natural fiber socks, laden with sweat, should keep feet drier? A program was initiated to answer not only this question, but also define which of the three most commonly used fibers is functionally best for athletic socks.

The first test involved 69 basketball players from 5 local high schools during their 60–120 min practice sessions under ambient conditions of 20–22°C (68–71°F) and relative humidities of 34–38%. From the literature, we estimate that the metabolic rate of this activity is 350–400 kcal/hr m^2. Each player wore one or more socks of Orlon®* on one foot and the same number of cotton or wool socks on the other foot. These were commercial socks with the Orlon and cotton being equivalent in yarn count and construction (terry cushion); wool was not available with a terry cushion. Note that the players did not know the fiber content of the socks. At the conclusion of the practice sessions, each player was asked which sock he preferred and why. The percent sweat gained was determined by weighing the socks before and after.

The experimental results, summarized in Table I show that 33 of the 40 players preferred Orlon versus cotton and 26 out of 29 preferred Orlon versus wool. Basically, Orlon was preferred because it kept feet drier and felt softer.

Table I. Athletic Socks—Field Test Preference

60–120 Min Basketball Practice with Delaware High Schools

School	No. of Players	O	C	W
		Preference		
A	14	11	2	1
B	10	10	0	0
C	18	14	3	1
D	14	12	1	1
E	13	12	1	0
Total	69	59	7	3

Summary

Overall, 59 out of 69 preferred Orlon acrylic versus cotton and wool:

- 33 out of 40 preferred Orlon versus cotton because it felt drier and softer

- 26 out of 29 preferred Orlon versus wool because it felt drier and softer

---

*Registered trademark of E. I. duPont de Nemours and Company, Wilmington, Delaware.

Table II summarizes the average percent sweat gained by all the socks tested and confirms that the natural fibers do absorb more sweat than Orlon.

Table II. Average Percent Sweat Gained by All Socks

Fiber	No. of Players	Socks	Average % Sweat Gained
Orlon	69	156	13.3
Cotton	40	89	22.2
Wool	29	67	27.1

Summary — Regardless of the number of socks worn on each foot, Orlon gained less sweat than the natural fibers.

However, since the Orlon sock gains less sweat, how is it possible for it to keep the foot drier than the natural fibers which gain more? Two hypotheses are: (1) the foot covered by Orlon is sweating less or; (2) Orlon transports sweat from the foot at a higher rate than the natural fibers.

To test the first hypothesis, two iron-constantin thermocouples were taped to each foot, with one foot covered with an Orlon sock and sneaker and the other by cotton or wool sock and sneaker. Nine athletes were asked to run in place for 15 min at a rate of 120–140 steps/min $\approx$ 175 kcal/m^2 hr. Temperature profiles were recorded for each thermocouple on each foot. Table III summarizes maximum foot temperature and temperature increase after 15 min and shows that there are no differences as a function of fiber type and confirms similar work by Carrie (1971). Using the energy balance equations of Fanger (1970), we conclude that equal skin temperatures require equality for water vapor diffusion through the skin and sweat secretion. In other words, the first hypothesis is not correct; both feet are producing the same amount of sweat.

The second hypothesis was tested by taping Drierite, which is blue when dry and pink when wet, to the outside of the sneakers at two locations. Eight athletes, wearing an Orlon sock on one foot and a cotton or wool sock on the other foot were asked to run in place at 160–180 steps/min ($\approx$ 200 kcal/m^2 hr) until the Drierite changed color. Note, the ambient conditions required to keep Drierite blue were 21°C/20% RH. Table IV shows that the time for the indicator to turn pink on the sneaker covering Orlon was five minutes. It took 12–15 minutes for it to change color when covering cotton and wool, respectively. Similar results were obtained with leather sneakers. This test not only supports the second hypothesis, but shows that Orlon is transporting sweat to the sneaker surface at a rate $\sim$ 2.5X faster than the natural fibers.

It is apparent that while running, the constantly changing mass of air surrounding the sneaker surface leads to a high rate of evaporation. Orlon

Table III. Foot Temperatures While Running

Running in Place—120-140 Steps/Min @ 21°C (70°F)/20% RH

Temperatures $^\circ$F ± 0.4

Subject[a]	Cotton Maximum	Δ	vs	Orlon Maximum	Δ
1	93.7	5.0		93.9	5.2
2	99.4	10.8		99.0	10.6
3	93.0	7.5		92.7	7.2
4	93.0	7.0		91.6	6.5
5	88.7	3.8		89.1	3.4
6	93.1	8.7		93.6	8.5
7	87.8	3.3		87.8	3.3
	Wool		vs	**Orlon**	
8	93.8	5.8		93.6	5.9
9	90.6	4.7		90.5	4.4

Conclusion — Maximum foot temperature is the same regardless of fiber type. Therefore, both feet are producing equal amounts of sweat.

[a]Subjects 1–3 wore leather sneakers, 4–9 canvas.

Table IV. Sweat Removal Rates of Athletic Socks

Running in Place—160-180 Steps/Min @ 21°C (70°F)/20% RH

Time for Drierite to Turn Pink (Min)

	Orlon	Natural Fibers
Canvas Sneaker	5	Cotton 12-15
	5	Wool 15
Leather Sneaker	5	Cotton 13
	5	Wool 15

Summary — Orlon is transporting sweat to the sneaker surface at a rate $\sim$2.5X greater than natural fibers.

transports sweat from the foot to the surface at a higher rate versus cotton and wool because we hypothesize that its higher surface energy leads to faster sweat transport via capillary action; and have measured a ten-fold lower sweat retention for Orlon. A demonstration of the unique ability of Orlon to transport moisture rapidly can also be made in the laboratory by measuring the time it takes for a piece of fabric to pump a known mass of water from a reservoir. For example, it takes 5 hr for a 15.2 cm x 2.5 cm (6 in. x 1 in.) piece of Orlon fabric, cut from the foot part of the sock, to pump 2 grams of water from a beaker, whereas the equivalent cotton and wool fabrics takes 10.5 and 13 hr, respectively.

Figure 2 graphically summarizes the mechanism we propose whereby Orlon keeps feet drier than the natural fibers. Sweat is drawn into the structure of the natural fibers and held tenaciously, whereas Orlon, which absorbs less sweat and has lower retention, continually transports sweat to the sneaker surface where it readily evaporates. Hence, drier feet should lead to reduced blistering (Comaish, 1971; Naylor, 1955).

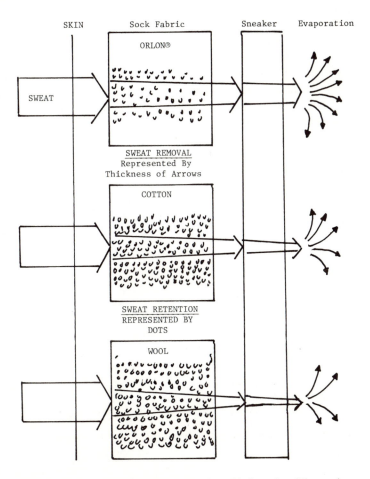

Figure 2. Mechanism of sweat transport by athletic socks while running.

THE EFFECT OF TACTILE AESTHETICS AS A PSYCHOLOGICAL STIMULUS

Fabric preferences for women's combination double-knit dresses, men's combination double-knit slacks and men's single-knit T-shirts were chosen as a vehicle to deal with the psychological stimulus of tactility. Tactile aesthetics were varied by changing fiber content. Preference was established by panels of men and women who compared the garments under controlled environmental conditions and during normal wear. Recognizing that there are many other variables which can determine or influence preference, all garments were the same style and color and altered, as required, to fit acceptably. Fabric construction for each end-use was identical; fabric weight and stretch differed by less than 5%.

In addition to conducting *garment* wear tests, blindfold tactile aesthetics preference tests were also carried out on the *fabrics* which went into the garments. For example, a woman was asked which of the three test fabrics (hidden behind a screen) she would prefer to wear most and least as a *dress* in the *summer* and the reasons for her choice. Thus, this tactile test requires: (1) fabrics, (2) a statement of intended end-use and season, and (3) preference based on tactile sensations only.

Because fabric physical properties also changed with aesthetics as fiber composition was varied, how well their physical properties predict preference will be summarized later.

Table V defines fabric construction and composition by fiber type and denier. In the case of the double-knit fabrics, the tactile aesthetics of the

Table V. Fabric Definitions

Double Knits – 56 Needles/cm (22 Needles/inch), Package Dye

- Dresses – 217 g/m^2 (6.4 oz/yd^2)

20%	80%	I.D.
100–34 ST Polyester	150–34 ST Poly.[a]	P
100–34 ST Polyester	150d Orlon	O
100–34 ST Polyester	150d–68 Taslan® Textured Poly.[a]	T

- Slacks – 244 g/m^2 (7.2 oz/yd^2)

20%	80%	
100d–20 ST Polyester	150d–34 ST Poly.[a]	P
100d–20 ST Polyester	150d Orlon	O
100d–20 ST Polyester	150d–68 Taslan® Textured Poly.[a]	T

Single Knits – 56 Needles/cm (22 Needles/inch) 132 g/m^2 (3.9 oz/yd^2)

- T–Shirts

100% Cotton – 180d	C
50//25/25 Orlon//Poly[a]/Cotton – 180d	O

[a] Polyester.

100% set textured polyester control fabric has been changed by introducing a spun yarn of Orlon—which has fiber ends—and a spun-like yarn of Taslan® textured polyester which has fiber loops. The composition of the cotton T-shirt was changed by replacing every other end of cotton yarn by Orlon and blending polyester fibers with the remaining yarn.

Table VI summarizes test conditions, number of participants and experimental results. For comparative purposes, the garment which should be preferred, based on the thermal, moisture and air resistant properties of the fabrics, is also listed. It must be stressed that these predictions should be compared only to those established under the controlled environmental conditions because it is only in this case that we are certain that the clothing ensemble has remained constant. Clearly, the physical properties of the fabrics did a

Table VI. Summary of Preference Studies

Summer Conditions	Predicted Preference Based on Fabric Physical Properties	Subjective Preference[a]		
		@ 27°C/80% RH[b]	After 10 Normal Summer Wearings	Blindfold Fabric Tactility Test
Dresses	P or O	P $\geqslant$ T $\geqslant$ O	P $\geqslant$ T $\geqslant$ O	P > T $\geqslant$ O
Slacks	P	O $\geqslant$ T $\geqslant$ P	O $\geqslant$ T $\geqslant$ P	O > T $\geqslant$ P
T-Shirts	O or C	O > C	O > C	O > C
Winter Conditions		@ 27°C/20% RH	After 10 Normal Winter Wearings	
Dresses	T or O	O $\geqslant$ P $\geqslant$ T	O $\geqslant$ P > T	O > P $\geqslant$ T
Slacks	T	O > P > T	O > P > T	O > P > T
Strenuous Activity			Basketball Practice	
Athletic Socks	O > C > W		O > C > W	O > C > W

[a] > means statistically significant @ p $\leqslant$ .05. $\geqslant$ means numerically greater, but not t statistically significant.

[b] Each garment worn for 15 min while walking at rate of 2.5 miles/hr.

poor job of predicting garment preference. For completeness, the results established for athletic socks are also tabulated. In the six cases studied, the results show that tactile preference predicts preference both during normal wear and under controlled environmental conditions. The predictions are significant in three of these cases and suggestive in the other three.

In almost all cases, the reasons given for tactility and wear preference were the same; viz., cool, warm, soft, body and drape. Thus, one can simply state that if a person likes the way a fabric feels, he or she will almost always prefer to wear the resulting garment. It appears that people are able to relate fabric aesthetics to previous wear experience with similar fabrics and have developed certain expectations, including expected wash and wear performance. Thus, tactile aesthetics appears to be both a garment property and an important stored modifier. From a practical point of view, since garment wear testing is expensive and time consuming, one can use the blindfold fabric tactility test to screen fabrics and, thereby, reduce the number of wear test items.

To summarize, field testing and mechanistic studies of sweat transport show that Orlon provides a better athletic sock than cotton or wool because it keeps feet drier. In the selection of "everyday garments," tactile aesthetics preference turned out to be the single most important parameter governing its selection provided all other criteria in Comfort's Gestalt were satisfied. Aesthetics is a property of the garment and a stored modifier of the wearer.

REFERENCES

Carrie, C. "The Effect of Man-Made Fibres on the Human Skin," *Third Shirley International Seminar: Textiles for Comfort* (June 15-17, 1971).

Comaish, J. S. and E. Bottoms. "The Skin and Friction," *Brit. J. Derm.* 84:37-43 (1971).

Fanger, P. *Thermal Comfort* (Copenhagen: Danish Technical Press, 1970).

Flugel, J. C. *The Psychology of Clothes* (London: The Hogarth Press, Ltd., 1950).

Fourt, L. and N. R. S. Hollies. *Clothing—Comfort and Function* (New York: Marcel Dekker, Inc., 1970).

Kemp, S. "The Consumer's Requirement for Comfort," *Third Shirley International Seminar: Textiles for Comfort* (June 15-17, 1971).

Naylor, P. F. D. "The Skin Surface and Friction," *Brit. J. Derm.* 67:239 (1955).

Pontrelli, G. J. Private Communications (1975).

Wilson, H. "Athletic Training—Blister Prevention," *Woman's Coach* (January 1975).

SECTION III

COMFORT SENSATION AND ASSESSMENT IN CLOTHING FABRICS

Chapter 7

PSYCHOPHYSICAL AND NEUROPHYSIOLOGICAL
STUDIES OF TACTILE SENSIBILITY

Robert H. LaMotte

Department of Physiology
School of Medicine
The Johns Hopkins University
Baltimore, Maryland 21205

The state of physical comfort may be greatly influenced by tactile and thermal sensations arising from contact between the skin and the immediate environment. Sensory receptors and associated neural pathways provide the only way in which the brain can obtain information about the outside world. Therefore, one useful way to study sensation is to correlate neurophysiological events originating in the receptors with behavioral measures of sensation.

A series of experimental studies of the touch-pressure sense in humans and other primates was initiated over 15 years ago by Dr. Vernon Mountcastle and his colleagues at The Johns Hopkins University School of Medicine. These investigations have followed a four-step approach to the study of mechanoreception. The same approach can be applied to the study of any sensory modality when the experimenter wishes to relate changes in physical energy delivered to the observer to physiological and behavioral events occurring within that observer. The first step is to specify, quantitatively, the physical dimension or continuum along which the experimental stimuli will vary. As an example, we might indent the skin with an electromechanical device and describe the continuum in terms of the number of microns of skin indentation; or, we might measure the force between the skin and stimulator device. The second step is to relate the stimulus changes, measured along a physical dimension, to the sensations they evoke measured along some psychological scale. That is, we might determine the minimal indentation of the skin which the observer can reliably detect 50% of the time. This minimal intensity is called his *detection threshold.* We might also determine the relationship between the amount of skin indentation and the subjective magnitude of the pressure sensations by asking the observer to rank the stimuli along a subjective intensive continuum, thereby producing a scale of subjective intensity. The third step in this approach is to use neurophysiological methods to determine the relationship between these same physical stimuli and electrical signs of activity recorded from single nerve fibers terminating in or beneath the skin. A corollary and obviously more complex problem is to investigate how the primary information conveyed along sensory pathways is processed by the brain to produce behavioral output in the form of sensory performance. Finally, the fourth step is to correlate sensory performance with the events observed within the nervous system, using in each case the same set of experimental stimuli.

Most of our physiological experiments are performed on the monkey, since his skin and peripheral nervous system are anatomically similar to that of the human. Consequently, whenever possible, we make behavioral measurements of sensory capacities in monkeys as well as in humans. When these capacities are shown to be the same for the two species, we can infer with greater confidence that the neurophysiological mechanisms we observe in monkeys are also present in man.

All sensations of touch-pressure, including complex ones such as roughness and pattern, arise as a result of displacements of skin. The amount of each displacement as well as its direction, rate and pattern are all physical parameters which can be studied. They are all important when the surface of an object is pressed against or moved across the skin. A practical strategy is to study the responses of primary afferent nerve fibers to stimuli which vary along only one or two known physical dimensions in order to obtain an unambiguous relationship between stimulus and neural response. For this reason, we have used an electromechanical device (Werner and Mountcastle, 1965) which displaces the skin a known amount in a *vertical* direction by delivering a mechanical step-indentation or a step with a mechanical sinusoid superimposed. A displacement transducer and feedback circuitry make it possible to maintain a desired displacement despite any variations in skin resistance, up to 1.5- to 2-mm indentations.

Figure 1 shows a cross section through the smooth skin of the human hand. Beneath the epidermis are the sensory receptors. It is the terminal ending of a peripheral nerve fiber which is differentially sensitive to one class of stimuli—that is mechanical, thermal, or noxious stimuli. Indirect evidence suggests that well organized structures encapsulate the endings of certain myelinated mechanoreceptive nerve fibers. These structures influence the dynamic response properties of the receptor but not its modality specificity. Three types for the smooth (glabrous) skin of the hand are shown in Figure 1:

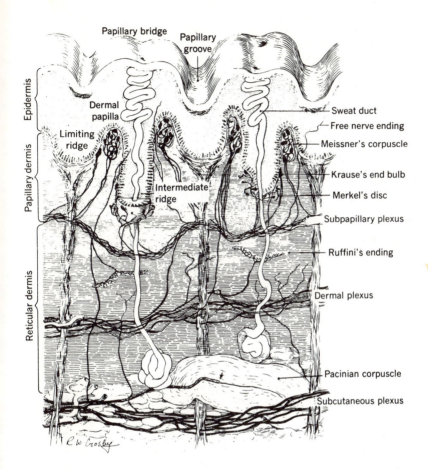

Figure 1. Vertical section through the glabrous skin of the hand. The skin consists of two main parts: (1) the *epidermis*—forming papillary ridges (with sweat pores) each separated by a papillary groove, and (2) the *dermis* which consists of a superficial layer called the *papillary dermis* and a deeper layer called the *reticular dermis.* Beneath the dermal layers is a layer of loose connective tissue, the *subcutaneous tissue,* which attaches the skin to underlying organs. Three major plexuses of nerves shown are the subcutaneous, dermal, and subpapillary plexuses. Three important types of nerve endings in the glabrous skin are: (1) *free nerve endings,* which are located throughout the dermis, may extend into epidermis and are the terminals of unmyelinated and probably small myclinated nerve fibers; (2) *Meissner's corpuscles,* which are encapsulated endings of larger myelinated fibers and are located within the dermal papillae; and, (3) *Merkel's discs,* which are expanded tips of the endings of myelinated fibers and are associated with the *intermediate ridge.* The latter floats freely in loose connective tissue not attached to the dermis. The *limiting ridge* is limited in its excursion of movement by fibrous tissue going to underlying bone and by an underlying, supporting longitudinal bundle of connective tissue (from Mountcastle, 1974). Figure 1 used by permission from Mountcastle, Vernon B.: Sensory receptors and neural encoding: introduction to sensory processes. In Mountcastle, Vernon B., editor: Medical physiology, ed. 13, St. Louis, 1974, The C. V. Mosby Co.; courtesy Dr. M. E. Jabaley.

1. *Meissner's corpuscles,* which are encapsulated nerve endings located within the dermal papillae and believed to be sensitive to mechanical movement against or across the skin;
2. *Merkel's discs,* which are expanded tips of a nerve ending, located at the surface of an intermediate ridge and putatively respond to steady or slowly changing pressure applied to the skin;
3. *Pacinian corpuscles,* which are onionskin-like encapsulations of the nerve ending, located primarily in subcutaneous tissue and very sensitive to high frequency vibrations.

There are other neuronal endings and one class of these is called "free nerve endings," because they are without encapsulations or expanded tips. These are the endings of small diameter myelinated or unmyelinated fibers thought to serve the pain and temperature senses.

When the nerve ending is activated by the appropriate stimulus, nerve impulses travel up the peripheral nerve fiber. These impulses are transmitted along the peripheral nerve into the spinal cord and then relayed to the brain. Schematic drawings of sections of the spinal cord and the brain are shown in Figure 2. Peripheral nerve fibers (sensory *afferents*) which terminate in or beneath the skin can be divided into two classes. The first class is the large diameter, myelinated fibers, which serve the mechanoreceptive modalities. The second class is the smaller diameter, myelinated and unmyelinated fibers serving the modalities of pain and temperature. The illustration shows a large myelinated mechanoreceptive fiber terminating in a Meissner corpuscle and an unmyelinated nociceptive fiber ending freely between tissue cells. While both classes of sensory afferents have their cell bodies within the dorsal root ganglia, they project their axons to different locations within the spinal cord. Many of the large, myelinated afferents ascend within the dorsal columns of the spinal cord and terminate within the dorsal column nuclei. Second-order neurons which originate in these nuclei project their axons across the midline and terminate in the thalamus. Third-order cells originating in the thalamus send their axons to the cerebral cortex.

The small myelinated and unmyelinated afferents which serve temperature and pain modalities enter the spinal cord and terminate within the dorsal horn of the spinal gray near their point of entry. Spinal relay neurons send their axons across the midline, ascend within the anterolateral funiculus and project to one or several areas within the brainstem and thalamus. The latter regions project widely upon the cerebral cortex.

The only way that a sensory nerve fiber can convey information to the central nervous system is by the number and the pattern of its nerve impulses. A useful technique is to correlate the rate or pattern of nerve impulses with variations in some physical attribute of the experimental stimuli such as intensity. The electrical signs of nerve impulses arising from a single, isolated

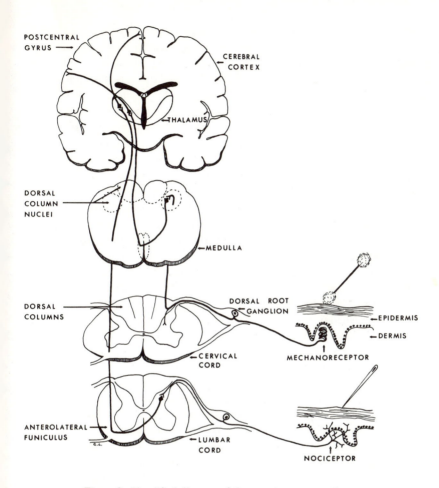

Figure 2. Simplified diagram of the somatosensory pathways.

nerve fiber can be observed electrophysiologically with a recording electrode. At a location several inches proximal to the nerve's termination within the skin, a small bundle of fibers can be dissected from the rest of the peripheral nerve and placed on an electrode. The localized region of the skin supplied by a single nerve fiber is called its *receptive field*; for mechanoreceptors innervating the glabrous skin of the hand, the receptive field is 2-3 mm in diameter. Appropriate stimulation of the receptive field of a nerve fiber results in one or more nerve impulses; the electrical signs of these impulses are picked up by the electrode, amplified and then displayed on an oscilloscope.

Experiments of this sort have revealed that mechanoreceptive afferents can be broadly classified into two types by the nature of their responses to steady mechanical step indentations of the skin. The *slowly adapting* fibers respond to a step indentation of the skin with an onset transient discharge which then declines to a fairly steady rate determined by the degree of indentation. This is shown for one such fiber in Figure 3. Each vertical line in the figure represents one nerve impulse. A voltage analog of the stimulus is shown beneath each discharge pattern and represents each of several skin displacements of increasing intensity. This class of mechanoreceptive afferents is believed to terminate in Merkel's discs. The second main class of mechanoreceptive afferents is called *quickly adapting* because their response to a steady displacement of the skin consists only of a brief burst at onset and removal of the stimulus. These afferents are especially sensitive to skin indentations which vary in time such as those produced by a mechanical sinusoid, or those produced by passing a fabric across the skin. Figure 4 shows the responses of two kinds of quickly adapting mechanoreceptive fibers to a mechanical sinusoid summed with a step indentation of the skin—the latter shown by the top trace for each record. In the upper half of the figure is the typical response of a quickly adapting mechanoreceptive fiber sensitive to low frequencies of oscillation in the 5- to 50-Hz range. Stimuli in this frequency range when delivered to the skin of human observers elicit sensations of "flutter." These mechanoreceptive afferents almost certainly end in Meissner corpuscles within the dermal papillae of the glabrous skin. I will refer to these as *"Meissner" afferents.* In the bottom half of the figure are the responses of another kind of quickly adapting mechanoreceptive afferent—one sensitive to high frequency mechanical oscillation in the 60- to 400-Hz range. Such stimuli elicit sensations of vibration when delivered to the skin of human observers. These fibers end in Pacinian corpuscles beneath the skin and I will refer to them as *"Pacinian" afferents.* Once the amplitude of a sinusoid is strong enough, the responses of these fibers become phase-locked or "tuned" to each cycle of the sinewave. On the top line of the figure, the sinewave amplitude is just below that required for tuning in a Meissner afferent. The next stimulus, below, has a slightly greater amplitude which elicits a tuned response of one impulse per cycle of the sinewave. The minimal amplitude required to elicit tuning is called the *tuning threshold* for the fiber. The minimal amplitude which evokes a minimum of only one impulse for the duration of the sinusoid is called the *absolute threshold* and is usually about one-third the amplitude required for tuning.

I will now describe some correlations that have been made between the results of psychophysical studies of steady pressure and flutter-vibration and the responses of the slowly and the quickly adapting mechanoreceptive afferents.

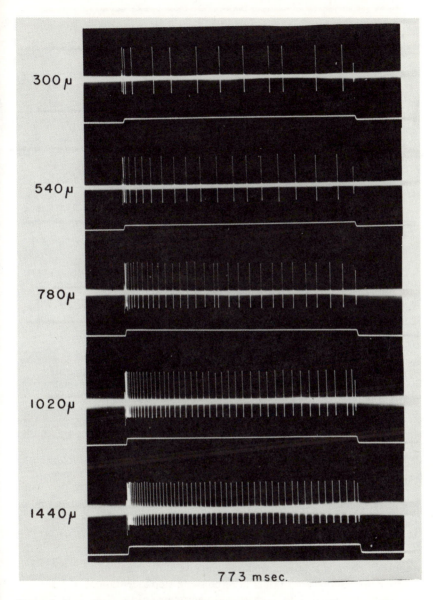

Figure 3. Recordings of nerve impulses evoked in a slowly adapting mechanoreceptive nerve fiber by mechanical indentation of the glabrous skin of the monkey hand. Each vertical line is a nerve impulse and a voltage analog of each stimulus is shown underneath each neural record. The net skin indentation is shown to the left of each record. The stimulus duration was 773 msec (from Mountcastle et al., 1966).

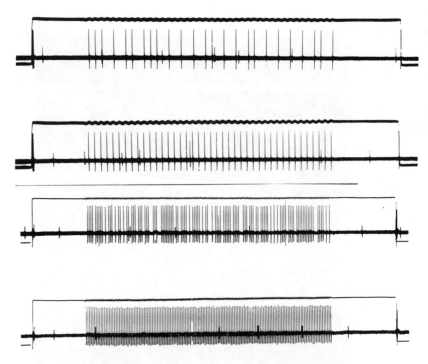

Figure 4. Records of nerve impulses in two types of quickly adapting mechanoreceptive nerve fibers innervating the monkey hand. The upper two records illustrate the responses of a "Meissner" afferent to a mechanical sinusoid of 40 Hz at amplitudes just below and just above tuning threshold for the fiber. The lower two records illustrate the responses of a Pacinian afferent to a 150-Hz sinusoid at amplitudes just below and above tuning threshold (from Talbot *et al.*, 1968).

PERIPHERAL NEURAL CODING MECHANISM FOR STEADY PRESSURE ON THE SKIN

The relationship between the degree of steady skin displacement and the responses of the slowly adapting mechanoreceptive afferents in monkeys (Mountcastle *et al.*, 1966) and humans (Knibestol and Vallbo, 1970) suggests the relevance of these fibers for sensations of steady pressure. Mountcastle *et al.* (1966) showed that the rate of discharge of a slowly adapting mechanoreceptive fiber in response to step indentations of 1-sec duration rises linearly with increasing displacements of the skin. It was subsequently shown that when human subjects were asked to rate these same stimuli along an intensive continuum by assigning numbers to them, the subjective magnitude of the pressure sensations also increased linearly with increasing displacements of the skin (Mountcastle, 1967). To what extent might this relationship between stimulus intensity and behavioral response depend upon "task" variables such as the psychophysical method used or the range of numbers chosen by the subject? I have recently repeated some of these experiments using three separate psychophysical procedures wherein subjects were asked to estimate the subjective magnitude of pressure sensations either by using a category rating scale of 1 to 15 or by using a scale of 1 to 30 (methods of "category estimation"). In a third procedure, subjects used numbers of their own choice based upon the perceived ratio of one intensity of pressure to another ("method of magnitude estimation"). Each procedural condition had 10 naive subjects. The same stimulus sequences, intensity values, durations and repetition rates used in the psychophysical experiments were also used in a set of physiological experiments. In the latter, stimuli were delivered to the receptive fields of slowly adapting mechanoreceptive afferents supplying the volar surface of the distal phalanx of the finger in monkeys. For both sets of experiments, 15 stimuli of 900-msec duration were delivered 10 times in a pseudorandom sequence with 8-sec interstimulus intervals using a 2-mm diameter probe tip on the stimulator. The left side of Figure 5 shows the average subjective estimates of pressure in humans under the three different psychophysical procedures as a function of skin displacement. Subjective estimates are expressed as the average of the percent of maximum judgement for each subject. Results show no differences between the procedures in the linearity of the relationship between estimates of subjective magnitude and physical intensity. The right side of the figure shows the stimulus-response functions of each of 10 slowly adapting mechanoreceptive fibers each fitted to a straight line by the method of least squares. Correlation coefficients were all between 0.90 and 0.99. The divergence of these lines suggests the way in which activity in the total population of mechanoreceptive fibers increases with increasing intensity of stimuli applied to the skin (Mountcastle *et al.*, 1966). The close similarity between the results obtained with different psychophysical procedures increases the generality of a two-fold proposition put forth by Mountcastle: firstly, that the neural transformations which intervene between the primary input from the peripheral nervous system and the final behavioral response (a judgment of subjective magnitude) are, in sum, *linear;* secondly, that the psychophysical relationship between physical and perceived intensity in the human observer is "set by the transfer properties of the receptors themselves" (Mountcastle, 1974).

Statements based upon an observed correlation between psychophysical measurements in humans and neurophysiological studies in subhuman primates depend upon a demonstration that the sensory capacities for the two species are similar. In the next section it is shown that this is indeed the case, at least for one aspect of cutaneous mechanoreception—the sense of flutter-vibration.

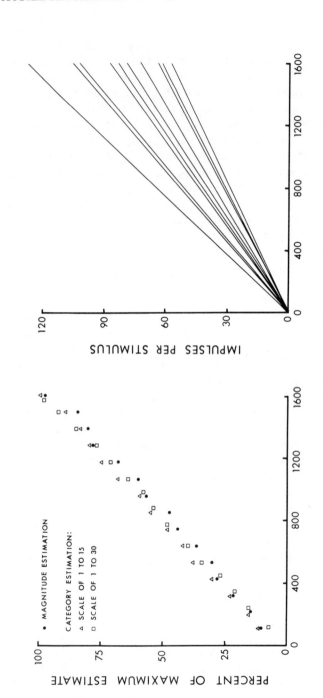

Figure 5. Results of subjective estimates of pressure by human observers (left panel) and stimulus-response relations of 10 slowly adapting mechanoreceptive fibers innervating the monkey hand. For both behavioral and neurophysiological experiments, the stimuli were step-indentations of 900-msec duration delivered every 8 sec in pseudorandom sequence to the distal pad of the finger. The probe tip was 2 mm in diameter, machined to one-third spherical surface. The intensity continuum was divided into zero and 15 equal steps with the maximum equal to 1600 μ indentation

PERIPHERAL NEURAL CODING MECHANISMS FOR
TEMPORALLY–ORDERED INDENTATIONS OF THE SKIN

The natural waveform of mechanical indentations elicited by movement of an object across the skin is very difficult to specify. We have therefore studied the responses of quickly adapting mechanoreceptive afferents to known amplitudes and frequencies of movement in the vertical direction. We correlated these responses with measurements of sensory capacities of humans and monkeys to detect and to discriminate between such stimuli (LaMotte and Mountcastle, 1975; Mountcastle *et al.*, 1972). Our first step was to determine by behavioral procedures the range of amplitudes and frequencies of mechanical sinusoids to which monkeys and humans were sensitive. As shown in Figure 6, we delivered these stimuli to one spot on the restrained hand of the subject. We rewarded the monkey with a drop of apple juice for releasing a

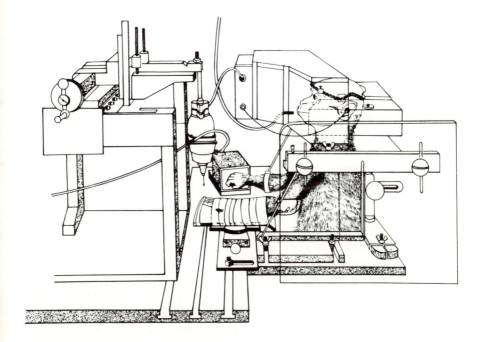

Figure 6. Drawing of the experimental setting used for psychophysical studies of the flutter-vibration sense in monkeys. The mechanical stimulator is shown just above the left hand which is restrained by tape in a plasticene mold. The right arm is also restrained but the hand is free to manipulate a response key. Liquid reward is delivered to the mouth by a feeder tube. The monkey faces a panel of lights which provide him with feedback about his performance (from Mountcastle *et al.*, 1972).

response key with the other hand when he correctly detected a vibratory stimulus. We varied the amplitude and frequency of these stimuli and obtained a behavioral sensitivity curve. These curves were determined individually for each monkey; several are shown on the right side of Figure 7. The minimal amplitude of sinewave the subjects could detect 50% of the time was determined at each frequency. These detection thresholds are plotted in Figure 7 for each subject at several test frequencies. The subjects are most sensitive to 200 Hz. Similar functions for human subjects, using the same stimuli are given to the left in Figure 7. The sensitivities to vibratory stimuli are virtually identical for monkeys and humans.

Next we compared the behavioral detection thresholds in monkeys and humans with the sensitivities of Meissner and Pacinian afferents innervating the glabrous skin of the monkey hand. We measured the absolute thresholds for a group of sensitive Pacinian afferents at several test frequencies; the results are plotted in the right panel of Figure 8 as closed circles along with the average behavioral sensitivity curve for monkeys. The Pacinian thresholds overlap the high but not the low frequency range of the behavioral sensitivity curve. We also determined the absolute thresholds for a group of sensitive Meissner afferents and these are shown in the left panel of Figure 8. Thresholds for these fibers overlapped only the low frequency range of the behavioral sensitivity curve. A corollary finding is that following anesthesia of the skin, the response capacity of the Meissner afferents and the capacity of humans and monkeys to detect low frequency stimuli are both completely lost or greatly reduced. At the same time, the sensitivity of Pacinian afferents beneath the skin and the capacity of monkeys and humans to detect higher frequencies are unaffected by cutaneous anesthesia (Talbot *et al.*, 1968; Mountcastle *et al.*, 1972). These results support the hypothesis that the necessary input to the brain required for the detection of oscillating mechanical stimuli is the appearance of minimal neural activity in these two populations of mechanoreceptors—those terminating in Meissner corpuscles in the skin for low frequencies and those terminating in Pacinian corpuscles beneath the skin for high frequencies.

What relevance might the tuning thresholds for these mechanoreceptive afferents have for sensory perception? Tuning threshold is about three times higher in amplitude than absolute threshold. Human observers report that mechanical sinusoids which they can barely detect do not elicit a sensation of flutter but only a vague feeling that a mechanical event has occurred. It is only when the sinewave amplitude is increased to about three times that required for detection that a clear sensation of pitch is felt. This suggests that the sensory capacity to perceive the periodic nature of a moving mechanical stimulus and to make discriminations between different frequencies of movement depends upon a periodic discharge in these mechanoreceptive

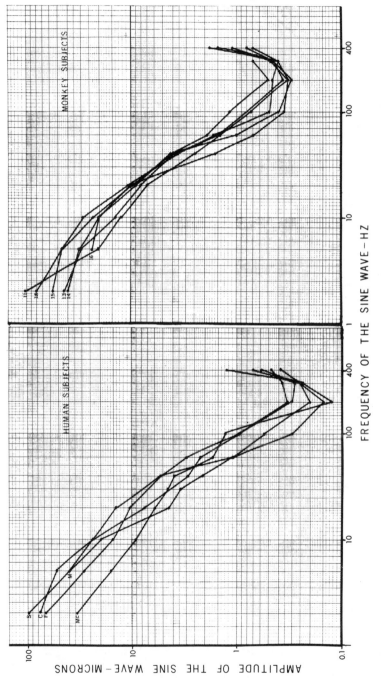

Figure 7. Frequency-threshold curves for six monkeys and five human subjects determined for sinusoidal mechanical stimuli delivered to the glabrous skin of the hand. Each point on each curve is the average detection threshold for that test frequency (from Mountcastle *et al.*, 1972).

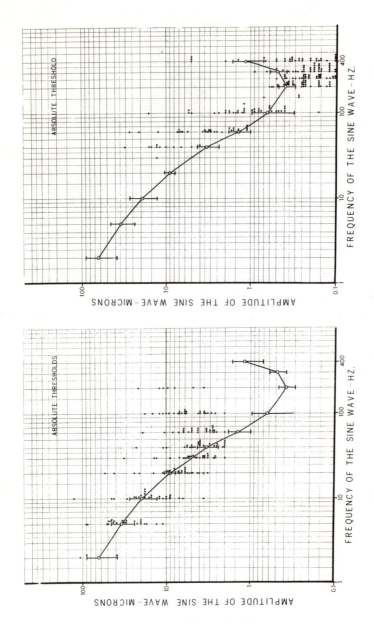

Figure 8. The solid line in each panel connecting open circles plots the average of the threshold curves for the six monkey subjects shown on the right side of Figure 7. Vertical lines are ±S.E.M. Filled circles plot the absolute thresholds for a group of Meissner afferents (left panel) and Pacinian afferents (right panel) at various test frequencies. The close correspondence between behavioral and neural thresholds suggests that the sense of flutter-vibration is served by these two sets of afferents (from Mountcastle *et al.*, 1972).

afferents, a discharge which is tuned to the pattern of indentations occurring on the skin. We have trained monkeys as well as humans to discriminate between mechanical sinusoids which differed only in frequency and not subjective intensities (LaMotte and Mountcastle, 1975). Their capacities to do so are excellent, for both species are capable of discriminating between stimuli which differ by less than 3 Hz. We made the assumption that frequency discrimination within the low frequency range is based upon differences in the periodicity of trains of nerve impulses in the Meissner afferents. From this, we predicted that if sinewave amplitudes were brought just below the tuning thresholds of the Meissner afferents the capacity to detect would be normal but the capacity for frequency discrimination would be lost. This is, in fact, what happens as shown in Figure 9. The probability of correctly detecting the presence of a 30-Hz mechanical sinusoid as a function of its amplitude is shown on the left for monkeys (solid line) and humans (dotted line). The two curves on the right of the figure show the probability of making correct frequency discriminations between a 30-Hz standard and other frequencies as a function of their overall amplitude. Psychophysical threshold for both tasks is arbitrarily defined as 50% correct. It is apparent that frequency discrimination is possible only at an amplitude level about eight decibels or slightly more than three times higher than that required for detection. This difference in amplitude between detection and discrimination thresholds we call the perceptual *atonal interval* since stimuli of amplitudes in this region do not elicit clear sensations of vibratory pitch. The left edge of the shaded region shows the average absolute threshold at 30 Hz for the population of Meissner afferents described in Figure 8, and the right edge shows their average tuning thresholds. These results support the hypothesis that detection of the faintest sensation of mechanical movement on the skin requires only minimal untuned activity in a small number of mechanoreceptive afferents. The capacity to recognize the pattern of movement or make frequency discriminations, however, depends upon the presence of a tuned pattern of nerve impulses in these same fibers. The similarity in sensory capacities of both species to detect and to discriminate between mechanical stimuli suggests that the neurophysiological events observed in monkeys occur in humans as well.

SPECULATION ON THE PERIPHERAL NEURAL CODING MECHANISMS FOR ROUGHNESS, SOFTNESS, AND SPATIAL PATTERN OF FABRIC SURFACES

How might the responses of the slowly and quickly adapting mechanoreceptive afferents be related to the recognition of softness, roughness, and other attributes related to the texture of fabric surfaces? It is well known that

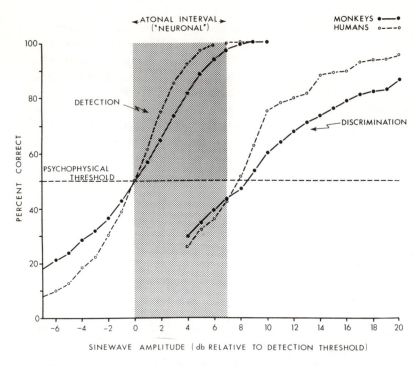

Figure 9. The atonal interval for the sense of flutter. Curves to the left represent the capacities of monkeys and humans to detect the presence of a 30-Hz mechanical sinusoid as a function of its amplitude. Curves to the right represent the capacities of either species to make frequency discriminations between 30 Hz and other frequencies as a function of sinewave amplitude. The dotted line defines the psychophysical threshold for both detection and discrimination tasks and is placed arbitrarily halfway between pure chance and perfect performance. The shaded area is the range of amplitude between the average absolute threshold at 30 Hz for a group of sensitive Meissner afferents (left edge) and that amplitude which elicits a tuned discharge (right edge) in these same fibers at 30 Hz (from Mountcastle *et al.*, 1972).

sensations of smoothness and roughness as well as the perception of surface pattern are greatly enhanced by movement of the object across the surface of the skin (Katz, 1925). Careful placement of the finger onto the surface of an object without movement in a lateral direction makes recognition of the texture or smoothness of its surface difficult. However, the sensations of softness and hardness of some materials still remain without lateral movements, for example the discrimination between foam rubber and wood. It is probable that judgments of softness, under experimental conditions allowing only vertical displacement of the skin, are facilitated by active movement. When pressing the skin against a surface, knowledge of the effort required to achieve a certain amount of skin indentation may complement information from the tactile senses. However, when movement is in a lateral direction the perception of roughness and texture or pattern does not seem greatly different whether the skin is moved over the textured surface or that surface is moved over the immobile skin surface (Katz, 1925).

In the following discussion I will not consider those physical attributes of a fabric such as compressibility and the diameter and length of any hairs projecting outwardly from its surface. I will assume that the surface of the fabric is completely described by the weave pattern and density and that it is woven with one kind of yarn. Perception of pattern and roughness is then likely to be influenced by the following parameters. Firstly, it will depend upon the amount of skin displacement occurring upon contact with the fabric. Within narrow limits, the greater the pressure applied by the skin, the rougher the fabric will feel. Both recognition of pattern and roughness certainly depend upon a minimal amount of pressure beyond that required to detect that something is there. This minimal pressure is analogous to the minimal amplitude of a mechanical sinusoid required for frequency discrimination and recognition of sinusoidal pitch. In fact, there may exist an "atonal interval" between the pressure required to engage a minimal irregular discharge in a few mechanoreceptive afferents, and the increase in pressure necessary to produce a "tuned" *spatiotemporal* pattern of discharge in a larger population of fibers. Secondly, perceived roughness and pattern depend in part upon *spatial frequency*—that is, the weave pattern and density. The greater the *yarn count* (*i.e.*, number of weft plus the number of warp per inch) the smoother the fabric will feel. In fact, one investigator has found a linear, inverse relation between judgments of the harshness of silk wool fabrics, and the square root of the number of weft per centimeter (Ali, 1971). Thirdly, the rate of lateral movement of the fabric with respect to the skin will also influence judgments of roughness and texture. Increasing the rate of movement probably increases the frequency of the displacement pattern, and this is analogous to increasing the yarn count when keeping rate constant. The higher the rate of lateral movement of the material's surface across the skin, the smoother it will feel (Katz, 1925). Finally, the diameter of the yarn in relation to the empty space between yarns may also influence its perceived smoothness and pattern. If spatial frequency or yarn count is held constant, one might predict that the wider and more closely the strands are woven the smoother the fabric will feel.

SOME OBSERVATIONS OF THE RESPONSES OF MECHANORECEPTIVE NERVE FIBERS TO STROKING THE SKIN WITH FABRICS

I have made some preliminary studies of the responses of mechanoreceptive afferents to stroking the skin with nylon fabrics. The fabric was fastened to a small plate which was displaced laterally back and forth on the skin over an extent of ± 2 mm at 4 Hz. The plate was tangential (parallel) to the volar skin of the distal phalanx of a monkey's finger. The plate was driven in a lateral direction by the same electromechanical device described earlier. The pressure exerted by the plate was varied and optically calibrated in microns of skin displacement. Skin indentation varied from the minimal value required to elicit one impulse per stroke (or less) to about 400 μ further into the skin. The total number of nerve impulses recorded from the fiber was cumulated over an 8-stroke stimulus of 1-second duration. Vertical displacement (skin indentation) was successively increased one step before each stimulus.

Figure 10 shows how a Meissner afferent increased its discharge rate in response to increased pressure of stroking. The two symbols represent the

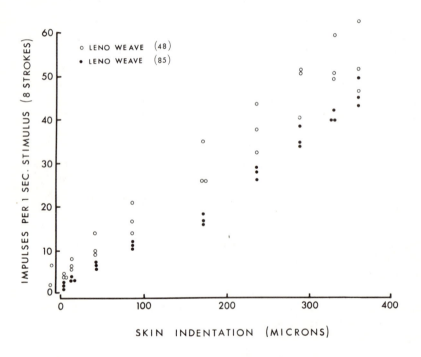

Figure 10. Stimulus-response relations for a quickly adapting mechanoreceptive ("Meissner") nerve fiber ending in the distal pad of the thumb of a monkey's hand. Stimuli were one of two nylon fabrics attached to a plate and displaced laterally ±2 mm at 4 Hz for 1 sec at each level of skin indentation. Indentation increased as an ascending staircase with each step preceding the next stimulus. Yarn counts are indicated in parentheses.

responses to two nylon fabrics which were very similar in construction and barely discriminable to human observers. The data represent three separate determinations of the entire stimulus response function derived for each fabric. Before each determination, the plate was removed, reattached, and realigned by eye. Despite some variability between successive measurements, the mechanoreceptor gave a greater response at all levels of skin indentation to the fabric with the lower weave density—the latter indicated in parentheses by the yarn count. Responses to either fabric were always greater than the response to the smooth, uncovered metal plate at comparable displacements of the skin (not shown in the figure). In contrast, Figure 11 shows the close similarity in responses of a slowly adapting mechanoreceptive afferent to a

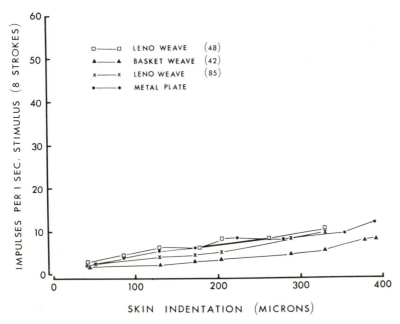

Figure 11. Stimulus-response relations for a slowly adapting mechanoreceptive nerve fiber innervating the distal pad of the middle finger of a monkey's hand. Stimuli were either a smooth metal plate or one of several nylon fabrics attached to a plate and displaced laterally ±2 mm at 4 Hz for 1 sec at each level of skin indentation. Indentation increased as an ascending staircase with each step preceding the next stimulus. Yarn counts are indicated in parentheses.

variety of fabrics, and a smooth metal plate. Again, as skin indentation increased, the discharge rate of the fiber increased slightly, but the stimulus-response relations provide little information upon which to base texture or roughness discriminations. This particular fiber remained somewhat responsive to lateral movement across the skin despite the continual indentation of the skin by the plate during and between laterally moving stimuli. Several other slowly adapting fibers "adapted" to this continual, steady pressure, and failed to respond to each successive stimulus.

> The Meissner corpuscles are located within the dermal papillae beneath the papillary ridges—an optimal location for selective response to minute pressure variations in a vertical direction produced by the lateral movement of a textured surface across the skin (see Figure 1). Cauna (1954) devised a mechanical model of a papillary ridge to show the function of the intermediate ridge (innervated with Merkel's discs) and of the papillary ridge containing Meissner corpuscles. In this model, the Meissner corpuscle is viewed as a spring, anchored by the limiting ridge, which, in turn, is fixed to the dermis. The corpuscle is best stimulated by pressure coinciding with its axis as opposed to oblique pressure. The elevated structure of the papillary ridge may limit the spread of a local stimulus as well as directing it to the underlying corpuscle(s) (Cauna, 1954). The intermediate ridge, which is not anchored to the dermis "follows the movements of the papillary ridge acting as a magnifying lever mechanism for transmission of touch stimuli to underlying receptors" (Cauna, 1954). These receptors (Merkel's discs) are viewed as responsive to pressure in any direction—oblique or otherwise—and therefore are not as selective in their responses as are the Meissner corpuscles. Textured material applied with steady pressure for a period of several minutes before being moved laterally might adapt some (not all) slow adaptors (although continual steady pressure does not seem to prevent perceptual recognition of texture). The quickly adapting Meissner mechanoreceptors, however, would still respond to local pressure variations brought about by protrusions in the material's surface as they moved across the papillae.

Three human observers were asked to rank numerically the roughness of a series of readily discriminable fabrics. The same materials as well as the uncovered metal plate were applied to the receptive fields of Meissner afferents. The results for one fiber are shown in Figure 12. The cumulative nerve impulse count during each stimulus increased as a function of increasing skin indentation. For any given level of skin indentation, however, the impulse count generally increased as a function of decreasing yarn count—the latter indicated by the first number in each parenthesis. This relationship was correlated with the ranking of the perceived roughness of the same fabrics, indicated by the second number in each parenthesis (5 = the roughest). In general, the lower the yarn count, the rougher the fabric felt. A minor exception was the fabric with the basket weave. It has a slightly lower yarn count (42) than a leno weave (48) yet was perceived as slightly smoother and evoked a slightly lower impulse count. A possible reason for this is the closeness of weave; the basket weave has yarns of 0.05 in. in width with no space between yarns. Each yarn in the leno weave was 0.01 in. wide and separated by slightly more than 0.03 in. of empty space. It is possible that perceived

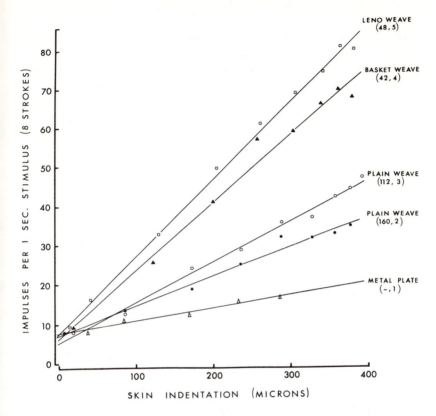

Figure 12. Stimulus-response relations for a quickly adapting mechanoreceptive
("Meissner") fiber ending in the distal pad of the middle finger of a monkey's hand.
Stimuli were a smooth metal plate or one of various nylon fabrics attached to a
metal plate and displaced laterally ± 2 mm at 4 Hz for 1 sec at each level of skin indentation. Indentation increased as an ascending staircase with each step preceding
the next stimulus. In parentheses are the yarn count (left) and subjective ranking of
roughness (right) associated with each material (5 = the roughest, 1 = the smoothest).

roughness increases with increases in the ratio of interyarn space to yarn
width.

These data suggest a peripheral neural coding mechanism for roughness
by the inverse relationship between perceived roughness (or nerve impulse
count) and weave density, when the level of skin indentation is held constant.
The data predict a monotonically increasing relation between perceived
roughness and skin indentation when weave density is held constant. The
exact nature of these relationships awaits construction of textile materials
with controlled spatial frequencies, which are delivered to the skin with better
control over force and displacement than available in these pilot experiments.

The spatial pattern of the surface of an object is probably encoded in the temporal and spatiotemporal pattern of nerve impulses evoked in the population of peripheral nerve fibers when the object is moved across the skin. In the present series of experiments, the pattern of nerve impulses evoked in a single fiber changed with variations in skin indentation, rate of movement and angular position of the stimulus. In contrast, the perception of spatial pattern (as opposed to roughness) in human observers remains invariant with small changes in pressure, rate of movement and angular position against the skin. Thus, a major role of central neural mechanisms in the somatosensory system may be to "sharpen up" the spatiotemporal patterns of activity in the peripheral nerve fiber population in order to extract the invariant "spatial features" of an object. Kirman (1973) has asserted that the tactile sense is highly specialized to process *coherent* spatiotemporal patterns. The tactile sense responds poorly when required to identify successive stimuli not related to one another as in a task requiring localization of discrete punctate stimuli. This has been a major weakness of many tactile communication systems designed to help the blind. In contrast, "if successive spatial patterns presented to the skin surface are close enough together in time and coherently related to one another configurationally, they are integrated into durable perceptual objects . . ." (Kirman, 1973). On a microscale, such patterns of pressure variations may occur within successive overlapping receptive fields of Meissner afferents as a textured surface moves across the finger tip. This may set forth coherently related spatiotemporal patterns of nerve impulses in the relevant population of peripheral nerve fibers.

It is possible that simple textile materials if properly constructed could be used by the neurophysiologist as experimental stimuli with which to study peripheral and central neural mechanisms of spatiotemporal processing in the tactile sense. Results of such experiments might also prove relevant to the study of tactile comfort. Feelings of comfort or discomfort are reactions to sensory states, which, in turn, can be psychophysically related to physical stimuli applied to the skin. The results of neurophysiological experiments can bridge the gap between the physical and behavioral states by defining the relevant first-order neuronal input to the central nervous system upon which a central processing mechanism must operate to create the sensory and behavioral response.

ACKNOWLEDGMENTS

I would like to thank Drs. Carole LaMotte, A. Georgopoulos, and J. Lynch for their assistance.

REFERENCES

Ali, M. A. "Factors Affecting the Softness of Silk-Wool Fabrics," *Pakistan J. Sci. Ind. Res.* 14:434-438 (1971).

Cauna, N. "Nature and Functions of the Papillary Ridges of the Digital Skin," *Anat. Rec.* 119:449-468 (1954).

Katz, D. "Der Aufbau der Tastwelt," (Leipzig: *Barth*, 1925).

Kirman, J. H. "Tactile Communication of Speech: A Review and An Analysis," *Psych. Bull.* 80:54-73 (1973).

Knibestol, M. and A. B. Vallbo. "Single Unit Analysis of Mechanoreceptor Activity from the Human Glabrous Skin," *Acta Physiol. Scand.* 80:178-195 (1970).

LaMotte, R. H. and V. B. Mountcastle. "Capacities of Humans and Monkeys to Discriminate between Vibratory Stimuli of Different Frequency and Amplitude: A Correlation between Neural Events and Psychophysical Measurements," *J. Neurophysiol.* 38:539-559 (1975).

Mountcastle, V. B., W. H. Talbot and H. H. Kornhuber. In: "Ciba Foundation Symposium on Touch, Heat, and Pain," A. V. S. de Reuck and J. Knight, Eds. (London, J. & A. Churchill, Ltd., 1966), pp. 325-351.

Mountcastle, V. B. In: "The Neurosciences. A Study Program," G. C. Quarton, T. Melnechuk and F. O. Schmitt, Eds. (New York: The Rockefeller University Press, 1967), pp. 393-408.

Mountcastle, V. B., R. H. LaMotte and G. Carli. "Detection Thresholds for Vibratory Stimuli in Humans and Monkeys: Comparison with Threshold Events in Mechanoreceptive Afferent Nerve Fibers Innervating the Monkey Hand," *J. Neurophysiol.* 35:122-136 (1972).

Mountcastle, V. B. In: "Medical Physiology," V. B. Mountcastle, Ed., Volume 1, (St. Louis: The C. V. Mosby Company, 1974), pp. 299 and 330-331.

Talbot, W. H., I. Darian-Smith, H. H. Kornhuber and V. B. Mountcastle. "The Sense of Flutter-Vibration: Comparison of the Human Capacity with Response Patterns of Mechanoreceptive Afferents from the Monkey Hand," *J. Neurophysiol.* 31:301-334 (1968).

Werner, G. and V. B. Mountcastle. "Neural Activity in Mechanoreceptive Cutaneous Afferents: Stimulus-Response Relations, Weber Functions, and Information Transmission," *J. Neurophysiol.* 28:359-397 (1965).

Chapter 8

PSYCHOLOGICAL SCALING IN COMFORT ASSESSMENT

Norman R. S. Hollies

Gillette Research Institute
Rockville, Maryland 20850

ELEMENTS AND RANGES OF OPERATION

Human perception of the world we live in involves all the senses and an unending series of concepts founded in the language we use to express these perceptions to one another. The process of making judgments from these perceptions is called psychological scaling and depends on the judgment scales we collect from experience and share with our peers throughout life. The importance of language or individual words in making perception possible is gradually becoming accepted in the fields of education and mental illness (Miller and Johnson-Laird, 1976). The psychological scaling process is best understood by referring to decision making in everyday life. Here are a few illustrations of common experience.

The ardent golfer, intent on making the most of his free time, will, on the morning of his game, proceed outside and from the appearance of the sky and the feel of the air make a quick decision on whether to go or not. Similarly, the man of the house may decide each fall when to turn off the air conditioner and make the furnace ready for winter heating. He makes this decision from the combined information of the current weather pattern, past memories of the weather and the immediate temperature cycles being experienced. Perhaps all of us can relate to the decision involved in buying a new pair of shoes. Once in the shoe store we consider the appearance, the cost, some measure of expected durability and performance and finally whether the shoes fit properly as we walk in them about the store. The range of subjects on which we can make useful judgments is never ending. We can and do judge the effectiveness of a speaker giving a technical talk. Manner of presentation, clearness of speech, organization of material and even charisma with the audience all operate to determine whether we consider the talk acceptable.

The application of psychological scaling to decision making in daily life is such a common human experience we are not particularly conscious of the steps required to carry out the process and make it useful as a form of study. Yet, by thinking through the examples just discussed or others which come to mind, there are at least six elements to psychological scaling which make it a useful discipline for scientific endeavor.

1. There must be a commonly recognized attribute or group of attributes to measure.
2. Language or terms to describe the attribute must exist.
3. There needs to be a scale assignment of two or more steps to represent the attribute level and its anticipated changes.
4. For a quantitative measure of the attribute, it is common to choose a rating panel and let them apply the rating scale to attribute measurement.
5. Data handling appropriate to the type of rating being made needs to be recognized and used.
6. It is often useful to compare the results from psychological scaling with objective measures of the same attribute.

Psychological scaling is used in a technical sense for many types of measurement of scientific and commercial value. Table I lists several of common experience in the field of textiles. Each is listed in terms of the subject being

Table I. Textile Uses of Psychological Scaling

For the Judgment of	Sensations Used	Type of Scale
Acceptable fabric hand	Dynamic feel and memory	Multiple scales
Fabric durable press	Appearance in standard lighting	Reference matching
Loss in fabric whiteness	Appearance under comparable lighting	Reference gray scale
Acceptable women's slacks	Appearance while being worn	Multiple scales
Grade of cotton quality	Appearance and feel	Multiple scales
Swatch color matching	Appearance in standard lighting	Reference matching

judged, the means of making judgments and the number and/or types of scales which are used in making the judgment. These examples illustrate two important features about psychological scaling as it applies to many different areas of measurement and in particular to textiles or clothing. The judgment may involve a single sensation but generally involves a combination of several sensations. The reference scales for judgment may have a physical counterpart such as durable press replicas, gray scales, and color charts or may have no simple physical counterpart such as the judgment of fabric hand, slack appearance, and cotton quality. The existence of a physical scale is not a requirement for making valuable, useful and precise psychological scaling measurements. Indeed, many aspects of comfort assessment of clothing items do not lend themselves to a useful physical model and so the application of psychological scaling to comfort problems does require a good understanding of the basis for the technique.

PSYCHOPHYSICAL LAWS AND DATA HANDLING TECHNIQUES

Some understanding of the history of psychological scaling is valuable in that it teaches the several variations which are possible in an approach to subjective judgment and further illustrates the reasons why some approaches are more useful than others. Although there is a long history of interest in psychological scaling, Table II shows that distinctive psychophysical laws have been proposed only a few times over the past 125 years. These workers,

Table II. Development of Psychophysical Laws

Worker	Period of Activity	Form of Law Developed [a]
Ernst Weber	1847–1878	$\dfrac{\Delta S}{S}$ = constant K
Gustav Fechner	1850–1887	$S = K \log R$
G. S. Fullerton	1892–1938	$\Delta S = MS^{1/2}$
L. L. Thurstone	1927–1954	$R_b - R_a$ = coefficient of correlation of S
S. S. Stevens	1936–1974	$\Delta S = KS^n$

[a] S = stimulus, R = response, K = constant, M = constant, n = constant.

primarily studying measurements by the human senses, separately, have described the detection of sensation as either increments of stimulus perceived by the observer, ΔS, at some stimulus level, S, or the response, R, detected by an observer resulting from a particular stimulus level, S.

Scales used for subjective measurement have been classified by Torgeson (1960) as shown in Table III and provide a good basis for determining which psychophysical law can be expected to apply to a particular scaling problem.

Table III. Types of Psychological Scales

	No Natural Origin	Natural Origin
No Distance	Ordinal Scale	Ordinal Scale with Natural Origin
Distance	Interval Scale	Ratio Scale

In a new area of study, the most effective approach is to use the simplest scale available for rating a particular attribute. This in turn dictates, as shown in Table IV, the mathematical base to employ and determines which statistical handling technique is appropriate to that data base.

Table IV. Data Handling Methods for Scales

Scale	To Determine	Math. Base	Acceptable Statistics
Nominal	Equality	$x' = x''$	Number of cases, mode
Ordinal	Greater or less	$x' = f(x)$	Ranking, median
Interval	Equal Differences	$x' = ax + b$	Standard deviation, mean
Ratio	Equal ratios	$x' = ax^n$	Coefficient of variation, mean

Development of the full potential of the ratio scale in Tables II, III and IV must be attributed primarily to Stevens (1951) who spent most of his life testing the bounds of human perception in many different areas of sensory science. The volume published in his honor (Moskowitz *et al.*, 1974) by several students and associates reflects to a small extent the substantial stimulation provided by Stevens to psychological scaling during his professional life. The individual wishing to further extend his understanding of psychological scaling, particularly in reference to the skin senses, is referred to the sources listed in Table V. The applications to clothing and comfort, however, are much less well documented, but, to the extent that they exist, are reviewed in the sections which follow.

Table V. Reference Texts on Psychophysiology and Psychological Scaling

1. Eccles, J. C., Ed. *Brain and Conscious Experience* (Cambridge: Massachusetts Institute of Technology Press, 1961).
2. Geldard, F. A. *The Human Senses* (New York: Wiley and Sons, 1972).
3. Guilford, J. P. *Psychometric Methods* (New York: McGraw Hill, 1954).
4. Guilliksen, H. and S. Messick, Eds. *Psychological Scaling* (New York: Wiley and Sons, 1960).
5. Kenshalo, D. R., Ed. *The Skin Senses* (Springfield, Illinois: Thomas, 1968).
6. Rosenblith, W. A., Ed. *Sensory Communication* (Cambridge: Massachusetts Institute of Technology Press, 1961).
7. Thurstone, L. L. *The Measurement of Values* (Chicago: University of Chicago Press, 1959).

APPLICATIONS TO THERMAL COMFORT AND WORK

The area of thermal comfort of man exposed to different combinations of clothing, climate and physical activity has been and continues to be a large and active field. Human perception of thermal comfort using psychological scaling has taken a variety of approaches tailored generally to a specific need. The early work of Yaglou (1925) which defined "effective temperature" as an index of warmth felt by the human body on exposure to various temperatures, humidities and air movements was found to have broad application. In this case the scale of effective temperature was fixed by the temperature of still saturated air which felt as warm as the given conditions. For example, any air condition has an effective temperature of 60°F when it feels as warm as still air at 60°F saturated with water vapor. The American Society of Heating and Ventilating Engineers for a time adopted Effective Temperature as the operating scale for establishing comfort charts of clothed individuals at rest and exposed to a variety of temperatures, relative humidities and wind velocities.

Over a period of years, workers in the John B. Pierce Foundation Laboratories and Kansas State University have extended this approach to many physiological and perceptual aspects of thermal comfort. More recently, Fanger (1970) has, with mathematical modeling, sought to define the neutral thermal comfort zone of men in different clothing and at different activity levels using mean skin temperature and sweat secretion rates as physical measures of comfort. A good deal of work has gone into determining whether men or women in different geographical locations are indeed subjectively comfortable under the conditions defined by the rather complex Fanger comfort equation. The American Society of Heating, Refrigerating, and Air-Conditioning Engineers (1974) presents generalized comfort charts based on Fanger's work for predicting comfort acceptance once the clothing, insulation, metabolic level, air temperature and wet bulb temperature or radiant temperature are defined.

Thermal comfort can be easily determined and readily applied using a simple linear scale such as that devised by John McGinnis of the Army Natick Laboratories and shown in Table VI. In the experience of the author such a

Table VI. McGinnis Thermal Scale

I AM:
1. So cold I am helpless
2. Numb with cold
3. Very cold
4. Cold
5. Uncomfortably cool
6. Cool but fairly comfortable
7. Comfortable
8. Warm but fairly comfortable
9. Uncomfortably warm
10. Hot
11. Very hot
12. Almost as hot as I can stand
13. So hot I am sick and nauseated

scale is readily applied in the field and is highly reliable for both thermal stress assessment and in severe climates as a check on subject safety (Hollies, 1971). In this case the subjective scale works well not only in hot and cold environments but either inside or outside the range of body temperature control by sweat evaporation.

Included in the work of Stevens (Hardy, Ed., 1963) were groups of studies to determine whether the detection of heat and cold formed a continuum of sensation as measured at the skin. Figure 1 shows the results obtained from asking a single observer to let the number 10 stand for the subjective warmth of an aluminum cylinder at 39.0°C presented inside the forearm followed by random presentations between 35.0 and 47.2°C. The equation of the line in Figure 1 converting degrees above neutral, °C, to degrees Kelvin, T_k, is

$$Sw = k\,(T_k - 305.7)^{1.6}$$

where Sw is the subjective warmth perceived. This information was thus readily expressed by the power law equation of Stevens (Table III) and corresponding studies below neutral temperature were equally consistent and displayed a power value of 1.0 confirming that cold and warm sensations were indeed perceived differently.

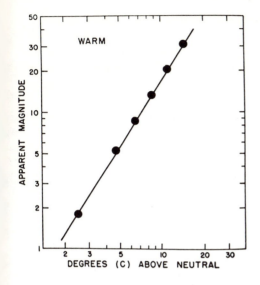

Figure 1. Perception of warmth on the forearm.

Exposure studies of men in the Antarctic during World War II led Dr. Paul A. Siple (1945) to develop a temperature scale for extreme cold which included the effect of wind. In this case a few measurements on men combined with many measurements on the cooling of a tin can in the cold resulted in the familiar Wind Chill Index of Figure 2. This is an example in which the results from psychological scaling and physical measurements were combined to achieve a useful guide to human cold perception and to provide safety limits for future use.

Apparent temperatures, °F, on exposed skin under windy conditions.
(For example, 20° with a 10 mph wind feels like 2°.)

Actual temperature:	30	20	10	0	—10	—20	—30
Wind, mph							
10	16	2	— 9	—22	—31	—45	—58
15	11	— 6	—18	—33	—45	—6C	—70
20	3	— 9	—24	—40	—52	—68	—81
25	0	—15	—29	—45	—58	—75	—89
30	—2	—18	—33	—49	—63	—78	—94
35	—4	—20	—35	—52	—67	—83	—98
40	—4	—22	—36	—54	—69	—87	—101

(Wind speeds greater than 40 mph have little additional chilling effect)

Figure 2. U. S. Army wind chill index.

In a similar manner, several attempts have been made to judge the work loads imposed on men, often combined with a stressful thermal load as it occurs in real life activities of precision or heavy work requiring more than usual mental or physical focus (Singleton *et al.*, 1971). Table VII shows the scale of perceived severity of work proposed by Dr. G. Borg (1971). Applied

Table VII. Scale of Perceived Severity of Work

20	
19	Very, very hard
18	
17	Very hard
16	
15	Hard
14	
13	Somewhat hard
12	
11	Fairly light
10	
9	Very light
8	
7	Very, very light
6	

to the problem of measuring the differences in ease of wearing different fire-coats, it has been useful in selecting optimum designs for working firemen (Hollies, 1973). This scale, like that of McGinnis (Table VI), permits maximum use to be made of human perception ability without the complications introduced by additional physical measurements of human stress. The application of such scales to real clothing problems teaches that scales which make maximum use of man's innate ability to perceive and measure complex phenomena turn out to be the easiest to apply and interpret for making quantitative measures of thermal comfort and work.

CONTACT COMFORT OF CLOTHING FABRICS

Although clothing is worn primarily for insulation and thermal protective purposes, the nature of clothing contact with the skin may be perceived in a number of different ways. The perception of wetness in next-to-skin clothing depends of course on the water content, which is easily measured, and on the type of contact with the skin, which is not so easily measured. Table VIII gives a subjective scale which was used by wearers asked to perceive wetness in shirting fabrics which were fluorocarbon-treated to change their rates of drying (Hollies, 1969). Surprisingly, as shown in Figure 3, the

Table VIII. Subjective Scale of Fabric Wetness

4	–	Wet
3	–	Moderately damp
2	–	Slightly damp
1	–	Dry

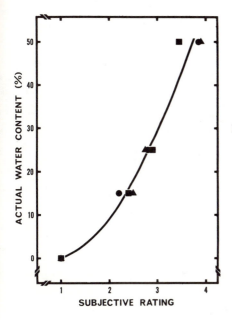

Figure 3. Evaluation of the wetness of fabrics with and without a fluoro-carbon quick-drying finish.

perceived wetness was the same for all the fabrics using a panel of raters. Thus, a single water content could be chosen at which all the fabrics would feel essentially dry.

Lundgren (1972) applied a similar approach to the psychological scaling of fabric hand (Stevens, 1951). His scale shown in Table IX was designed to allow the rater free choice in integrating the factors making up acceptable fabric hand. Separate measurements of three of the mechanical properties expected to influence fabric hand were then measured and compared with the subjective scaling results as shown in Table X. Clearly psychological scaling of this important but complex property was only partly related to these modes of fabric behavior.

Subjective scaling applied to the broader aspects of clothing contact comfort was found to depend on the water content of the fabrics in contact with

Table IX. Skin Contact Hand Scale

5	–	Excellent
4	–	Good
3	–	Moderate
2	–	Acceptable
1	–	Unacceptable

Table X. Fabric Stiffness, Roughness and Compactness
Compared with Subjective Fabric Hand

Fabric	Stiffness	Roughness	Compactness	Hand
C	0.474	0.223	0.425	2.6
D	0.495	0.215	0.417	3.0
E	0.376	0.219	0.364	3.3

the skin (Hollies, 1971). Figure 4 taken from this work shows a strong relationship between the water content of the clothing due to sweating, the water content of air or relative humidity of the comfort test room, and the subjective comfort rating (SCR) assigned to the garment worn.

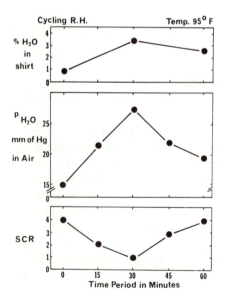

Figure 4. Subjective comfort rating of a cotton shirt at several levels of water in the air environment.

In further psychological scaling work, wearers were asked to describe the comfort sensations noted while wearing garments in a microclimate of varying temperature and relative humidity. Table XI summarizes the terms most often used by men and women in these tests and the means for recording perceived comfort intensities at regular intervals in the environmental chamber (Hollies, 1965). Knit shirts compared in this manner using the averages of

Table XI. Subjective Comfort Rating Chart

Comfort Description	Minutes in Environmental Chamber					
	0	15	30	45	60	75
Stiff	–	–	–	–	–	–
Staticky	–	–	–	–	–	–
Sticky	–	–	–	–	–	–
Nonabsorbent	–	–	–	–	–	–
Cold	–	–	–	–	–	–
Clammy	–	–	–	–	–	–
Damp	–	–	–	–	–	–
Clingy	–	–	–	–	–	–
Picky	–	–	–	–	–	–
Rough	–	–	–	–	–	–
Scratchy	–	–	–	–	–	–

Comfort Intensity Scale

1 — 2 — 3 — 4 — 5

Totally   Completely
Uncomfortable   Comfortable

comfort ratings from each comfort descriptor and data from three different intervals in the environmental chamber gave the results shown in Figure 5 (Hollies and Hall, 1975). In this way the subjective contact comfort ratings of shirts differing in cotton content and chemical finish could be meaningfully compared.

Figure 5 contains information on a second measurement employing psychological scaling to arrive at a fabric property. Cobaltous chloride as an anhydrate has a bright blue color. The hexahydrate, however, has a light pink color. Fabrics padded with cobaltous chloride solution and dried at room temperature undergo a change in surface color from blue to pink as up to 30% water is added (Hollies, 1975). Individuals observing fabrics padded with cobaltous chloride and subjected to increasing water contents can distinguish the colors listed in Table XII. The corresponding color index

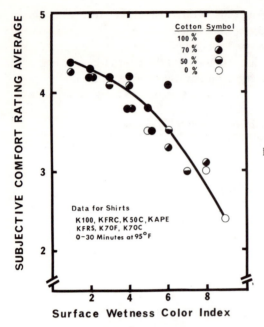

Figure 5. Relation of subjective comfort rating to the measurement of dynamic surface moisture.

Table XII. Surface Wetness Color Index for Knit Shirts Impregnated with Cobaltous Chloride

Color Index	Color Description
1	royal blue
2	medium blue
3	dull light blue
4	light blue — lavender edge
5	lavender blue
6	lavender
7	lavender pink
8	pink lavender
9	pink with lavender center
10	pink

numbers, therefore, represent perceivable increments in color and water content of fabrics containing cobaltous chloride.

This means for subjectively measuring fabric surface wetness was applied to the knit shirting fabrics of Figure 5 using a simulated sweating hot plate (Hollies and Hall, 1975). The hot plate and fabrics were placed in the environmental room used for comfort comparisons of the shirts on people. Colors of the shirting fabrics next to the sweating surface were observed at the same time intervals used in the comfort comparisons. These results are also given in Figure 5 and show good qualitative correlation with the subjective comfort ratings measured under the same microclimate conditions. The most obvious conclusion is that comfort acceptance of garments next to the skin is in some way related to the ability of these garments to remove sweat from the skin-garment interface. An equally important finding for the purposes of this paper was that psychological scaling could be used in both the comfort and surface moisture measurements to arrive at the overall conclusion. At this point in time, neither of these garment attributes can be measured by physical measurements alone.

FUTURE OPPORTUNITIES FOR APPLYING PSYCHOLOGICAL SCALING IN CLOTHING COMFORT PROBLEMS

From the examples presented in this chapter it is clear that many of the methods for applying psychological scaling to comfort problems are fairly well-established. The work further suggests that many aspects of comfort may not be resolvable as simple physical measurements of heat or moisture exchange or physical contact of clothing fabrics with the skin. This does not mean, however, that useful comparisons cannot be made or that the results will not be convincing on a sound statistical basis appropriate to each scaling technique used.

The word comfort is often used broadly to include clothing attributes beyond those of insulation and physical contact with the body. Many of these areas are particularly suited to the psychological scaling approach and perhaps deserve some attention by workers in the field. A partial list for future consideration might include the measurement of:

1. clothing appearance factors of style and fit,
2. the ease of working and living in ordinary clothing,
3. special clothing contact requirements for extreme environments,
4. clothing contact acceptability while working or when used in sports,
5. comfort assessment of shoes and socks while being worn,
6. effect of clothing color on comfort acceptance,
7. ease of glove use in cold weather clothing, and
8. effectiveness of yarn bulking on fabric contact comfort.

In each case for which a psychological scaling approach is chosen, it is important to obtain from the prospective raters the words and language of perception before deciding on the psychological scales of measurement and their appropriate intensity ranges. Experience has shown that the most meaningful psychological scale work has resulted from studies in which the observer is permitted free use of the language he considers appropriate to describe the phenomenon under study.

REFERENCES

American Society of Heating, Refrigerating and Air-Conditioning Engineers. *Handbook of Fundamentals,* Chapter 7 (New York: ASHRAE, 1974).

Borg, G., B. Edgren, and G. Marklund. "A Simple Walk Test of Physical Working Capacity," Report No. 18, Institute of Applied Physiology, University of Stockholm (1971).

Fanger, P. O. *Thermal Comfort* (Copenhagen: Danish Technical Press, 1970).

Hardy, J. D., Ed. *Temperature, Its Measurement and Control in Science and Industry,* Chapter 23 (New York: Reinhold, 1963).

Hollies, N. R. S. "Investigation of the Factors Influencing Comfort in Cotton Shirts," Final Report, Contract 12-14-100-7183, U. S. D. A., New Orleans (1965).

Hollies, N. R. S. "Development of Finishes for Cotton to Render Them More Rapid Drying," Final Report, Contract 12-14-100-8158, U. S. D. A., New Orleans (1969).

Hollies, N. R. S. "The Comfort Characteristics of Next-to-Skin Garments, Including Shirts," *Shirley International Seminar on Textiles for Comfort,* Manchester, England (1971).

Hollies, N. F. S., L. Fourt, G. Arnold, and N. Custer. "Use Type Tests for Comfort and Effectiveness of Firemen's Turnout Coats," Final Report, Contract 2-35929, N. B. S. (1973).

Hollies, N. R. S. "Cotton Clothing Attributes in Subjective Comfort," *15th Textile Chemistry and Processing Conference*, U. S. D. A., New Orleans (1975).

Hollies, N. R. S. and P. L. Hall. "Comfort Acceptance in Knit Structures," *AATCC Symposium on Sense and Nonsense in Knit Structures,* New York (1975).

Lundgren, H. P. Private communication, Dept. of Consumer Science, Univ. of California, Davis (1972).

Miller, G. A. and P. N. Johnson-Laird. *Language and Perception* (Cambridge: Harvard University Press, 1976).

Moskowitz, H. R., B. Scharf and J. C. Stevens, Eds. *Sensation and Measurement* (Boston: Reidel, 1974).

Singleton, W. T., J. G. Fox and D. Whitfield, Eds. *Measurement of Man at Work* (New York: Reinhold, 1971).

Siple, P. A. and C. F. Passel. "Wind Chill Perception," *Proc. Amer. Physiol. Soc.* 87:177 (1945).

Stevens, S. S., Ed. *Handbook of Experimental Psychology* (New York: Wiley, 1951).

Torgerson, W. S. *Theory and Methods of Scaling* (New York: Wiley, 1960).

Yaglou, C. P. and W. E. Miller. "Effective Temperature with Clothing," *Trans. Amer. Soc. Heat. Vent. Engrs.* 31:89 (1925).

Chapter 9

TECHNIQUES FOR THE SUBJECTIVE ASSESSMENT OF COMFORT IN FABRICS AND GARMENTS

John F. Fuzek

Research Laboratories
Tennessee Eastman Company
Division of Eastman Kodak Company
Kingsport, Tennessee 37662

R. L. Ammons

Eastman Chemical Products, Inc.
Subsidiary of Eastman Kodak Company
Kingsport, Tennessee 37662

INTRODUCTION

Before the introduction of synthetic fibers early in the 17th century, the fibers in general use were cotton and wool. Smaller amounts of silk and linen were also used. With the proliferation of synthetic fibers, the opportunity to make many intercomparisons between the performance of these fibers became available. One of the factors entering these comparisons was comfort. Some of the natural fibers have a reputation of being comfortable, while some of the synthetics have a reputation of being less comfortable.

For the purposes of this chapter, we define comfort as the sensation of contented well-being and the absence of unpleasant feelings. Furthermore, the tests and results described apply to the comfort or discomfort experienced in everyday living and not to the extreme environmental conditions, such as those encountered in tropical or polar expeditions.

We feel comfortable with that to which we are accustomed. For example, the individual who wears wool shirts says he is very comfortable with this shirt even in midsummer, while many persons wearing a wool shirt would say it was uncomfortable even in midwinter. This is a matter of considering the usual attire as being comfortable, and any deviation or change in that attire is considered uncomfortable. Another example is that of garments made from filament yarns. Approximately one-half of the population (women) consider these garments comfortable—at least they buy and wear them—while the other half of the population (men) generally find filament yarn garments to be uncomfortable.

The subjective assessment of comfort is dynamic, not static. It is constantly changing as we become accustomed to changes in fabrics, garments, styles, etc. When nylon hosiery for women first became available during and after World War II, it was deemed to be cold and uncomfortable, compared to the silk stockings then in common use. Today, we do not hear these comments, and nylon hosiery is the norm (Lynn, 1972). A wear test we conducted 5 yr ago on polyester T-shirts gave different results (subjective evaluation) from one conducted last year. These shirts were significantly more acceptable last year than they were 5 yr ago when the norm was 100% cotton. In view of these comments, it is obvious that comfort is a subjective phenomenon, difficult to measure by objective approaches.

Many objectively measured properties can be related to comfort, but no one parameter can be used in its total description. In fact, even the use of all of the known or suspected factors influencing comfort do not fully describe comfort. These objective factors considered in the assessment of comfort are thermal properties (conductivity, specific heat, emissivity), moisture properties (wettability, moisture regain, rate of moisture transfer, heat of moisture absorption), fabric characteristics (construction, hand, stiffness, smoothness), and fiber characteristics (staple length, crimp, diameter, modulus). Many other factors could also be considered.

EXPERIMENTAL

This chapter attempts to describe our techniques for subjectively evaluating comfort in garments and our attempts at correlating these results with objective test results. We have used two statistical methods—the random block design and Scheffe's (1952) paired comparison method—for the subjective evaluation of comfort.

The random block design in which each garment is evaluated by every participant offers the advantages of relatively easy data analysis with fewer participants, hence, easier data collection. On the other hand, this method gives more problems in evaluation to the participants, because they have to rate all of the garments in a particular test. Also, if a participant drops out of the test, the data analysis becomes much more difficult. A further disadvantage is the use of fewer participants giving a smaller sampling of the population.

The second method, that of Scheffé, is our method of choice. In this technique, each participant is issued only two garments for comparison. Because each participant has only two garments to rate, the subjective evaluation is easier. Because of the experimental design, a much larger number of participants is involved, giving a broader view of the ratings. Dropouts in the plan do not materially affect the data analysis; and finally, this experimental method results in completion of a wear test in a shorter time. The principal disadvantage to the method is the bookkeeping involved with the large number of participants. The number of participants required for testing N garment types is shown in Table I. Generally, several replications of each pair

Table I. Number of Paired Comparisons Needed for N Garments

$$P_r^n = n!/2(n-r)!$$

N	Number of Pairs
2	1
3	3
4	6
5	10
6	15
7	21
8	28
9	36
10	45
11	55
12	66

are required; hence, the number of participants can be large. For example, in a wear test involving 5 garment types, 10 participants are required for each replication. Since 10 to 15 replications are usually used, this test would require at least 100 participants. For such a test, each participant is issued two garments. This design is shown in Table II.

Table II. Paired Comparisons

Wearer	H	L	R	O	M
			Shirt Code		
1	X	X			
2	X		X		
3	X			X	
4	X				X
5		X	X		
6		X		X	
7		X			X
8			X	X	
9			X		X
10				X	X

Selection of participants is very important to obtaining reliable subjective data. It is essential that the participant normally wear the type of garment being evaluated. For example, in a T-shirt wear test, the participants must normally wear T-shirts. In addition they should wear T-shirts of the design being used in the test. (T-shirts come with V-neck or oval necks.) The participants should not be associated in any technical or professional manner or employed in areas associated with fibers, textiles, etc. The participation should be voluntary. We have found that participants who wear large or medium sizes are more sensitive to comfort factors than are small size wearers; hence, we restrict our participants to large or medium sizes. In our earlier wear tests we tried to use an equal number of plant workers and office workers in our tests; however, we have found that workers in environmentally controlled areas (air-conditioned) are more sensitive to comfort evaluation than are those workers employed in uncontrolled environments. The latter workers probably experience some discomfort most of the time and are hence less able to detect smaller differences in garment comfort.

In evaluating comfort of a garment, we have found that results can be influenced if the garments are not identical in appearance. We try to control color, garment fit and design, garment dimensional stability, fabric weight and thickness, and hand so that all of the garments under test are as close in these respects as possible (unless one of the parameters is a variable in the test).

Code letters or numbers used in a wear test are very important. Letters that have generally been found to be permissible are: D, E, G, H, M, O, R, S and T. Those letters to be avoided are: A, B, C, F, Q, X and Y. It has been found that if two identical garments are labeled A and B, participants in a wear test will show a preference for A by about a 60/40 ratio.

The questions asked of participants can result in misleading subjective data. We prefer not to lead our participants. They are unaware of the purpose of the wear test in which they are participating. We use the question "Which garment do you prefer and why?" This question is asked after one wear/wash cycle, after five cycles and after 10 cycles. After these questionnaires have been answered, we ask each participant to complete a more detailed questionnaire in which leading questions are asked. An example is given in Table III.

RESULTS AND DISCUSSION

Now we would like to discuss a wear test we carried out and some of the results we obtained. The objective of this wear test was to evaluate consumer acceptability of a fiber product in a T-shirt relative to the accepted article of commerce, and in particular, to determine whether comfort was a factor in the acceptance or rejection. This wear test was carried out in a random block

Table III. Questionnaire After Test Completion (10 Cycles)

Was the Garment

1. hot?		6. comfortable?
2. prickly?		7. clammy?
3. steamy?		8. cold?
4. soft?		9. stiff?
5. scratchy?		10. raggy?

11. Was the garment suggestive of women's undergarments?
12. Did the garment fit at the neck? ✓
13. Did the garment fit at the armholes?
14. Did the garment cling to you during wear?
15. Did the garment fit properly?
16. Were you aware of the garment during wear?
17. Was the garment hand (feel) satisfactory?

design with 24 participants (12 office workers/12 plant workers). Each participant was issued one shirt of each of 5 types. One of the T-shirts was the shirt generally in public use at the time of the test. Each participant compared two shirts/cycle in a random selection and sequence. Each participant wore all combinations. The wear test ran 10 wear/wash cycles per season. The tests were conducted in summer and winter. Each wearer thus wore each shirt for a total of 4 times per season. The participants answered a questionnaire after each cycle of wear/wash. The wear design is shown in Table IV.

Table IV. T-Shirt Wear Test Design

Wearer No.	Cycle No.									
	1	2	3	4	5	6	7	8	9	10
1	LO	RM	RH	RO	OH	LR	LM	OM	LH	MH
2	OH	LR	LM	RO	OM	MH	LO	RM	LH	RH
3	RO	OH	LH	MH	RM	LR	OM	LM	LO	RH
4	RH	OM	RO	LR	LO	RM	LH	MH	LM	OH
5	LO	LM	OM	OH	RM	RO	MH	LR	RH	LH
6	MH	RH	RO	LO	LM	OM	LH	OH	LR	RM
7	MH	LM	RH	OH	LO	RO	LR	ṘM	LH	OM
8	LH	OH	LM	RO	OM	RH	LO	RM	LR	MH
9	OH	LO	RH	LM	MH	LH	RO	OM	RM	LR
10	RM	LM	RH	OM	OH	LR	LH	LO	RO	MH
11	RO	OM	LO	MH	OH	LR	LH	LM	RM	RH
12	MH	LR	LO	OM	LH	RM	LM	OH	RO	RH

This design was used for the 12 office workers and duplicated for the 12 plant workers participating in the test. The questionnaire used for this wear test is shown in Table V.

Table V. T-Shirt Wear Test Questionnaire

	L Much Better	L Better	Same	R Better	R Much Better
Whiteness	☐	☐	☐	☐	☐
Feel of material	☐	☐	☐	☐	☐
Shape retention	☐	☐	☐	☐	☐
Wearing comfort	☐	☐	☐	☐	☐
Warmth	Hotter ☐		☐	Hotter ☐	
Comfort-absorption of perspiration		☐	☐	☐	
Clinging-static electrification	Less ☐		☐	☐	Less
Overall—which shirt do you prefer?		☐	☐	☐	

The overall preference is shown in Figure 1. Shirt H was the commercial product. These results indicate that there was no significant difference in acceptability among shirts L, R, O and H; but shirt M was definitely not preferred. Wearing comfort (Figure 2) showed a similar result for the summer phase; but for the winter phase, although again shirt M was not preferred, in addition shirt R was more comfortable than the control shirt H. Comfort due to the absorption of perspiration (Figure 3) showed similar data for the summer phase, *i.e.*, shirt M was not preferred and showed no significant difference among any of the shirts in the winter phase, probably because perspiration is not a problem in winter. Warmth (Figure 4) as a comfort factor showed about the same relationship among the shirts as did overall comfort for the summer wear test but less differentiation in the winter. The hand or feel of a shirt must be considered a comfort factor, since harsh, stiff garments

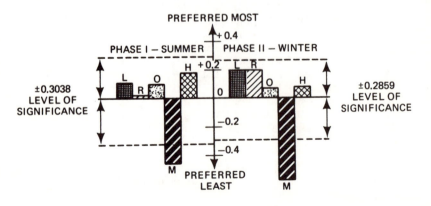

Figure 1. Overall preference of T-shirts.

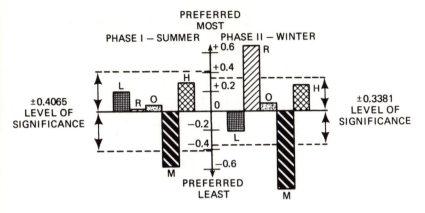

Figure 2. Wearing comfort of T-shirts.

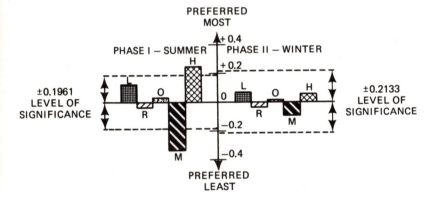

Figure 3. Differences in comfort due to perspiration absorption of T-shirts.

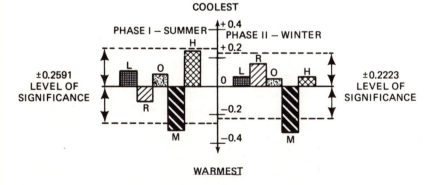

Figure 4. Differences in comfort due to warmth of T-shirts.

could cause discomfort: The preference of hand for the T-shirts evaluated
(Figure 5) was for shirt L over shirt M, but no significant difference was found
among shirts R, O and H. Static electrification as a comfort factor was also considered (Figure 6). During summer wear, when static is not a major problem,

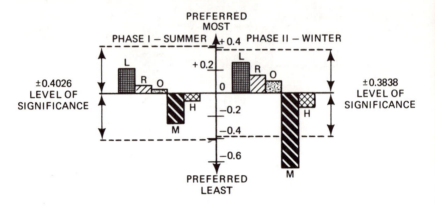

Figure 5. Feel of material of T-shirts.

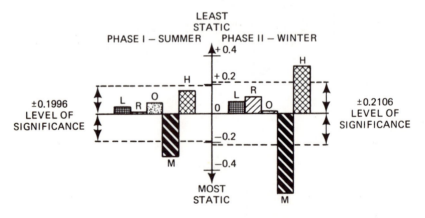

Figure 6. Comfort differences due to clinging or static of T-shirts.

there was no significant difference in the acceptability of shirts L, R, O and
H; however, during winter wear, shirt H was preferred over shirts L, R, O and
M. Softness and fullness of the shirts after 20 washes indicated that shirt H
was generally less preferred than the other shirts (Figure 7).

Correlation between the subjective factors obtained in this manner with
objectively measured test parameters are shown in Table VI as correlation
coefficients. These results indicate little correlation between the factors

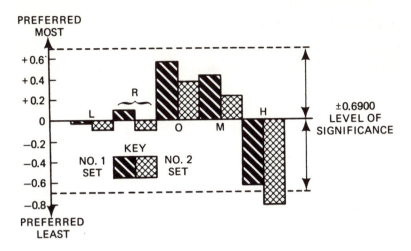

Figure 7. Softness and fullness of T-shirts after 20 washes.

**Table VI. Relationship of Subjective Evaluations vs Objective Test
Results—Correlation Coefficients**

	Objective Tests									
Subjective	MR	H₂O IMB	Wet	Wicking	MVT	Cling	Static	Friction	Tenacity	Modulus
Preference	70	62	52	50	58	39	03	-36	-20	-21
Hand	27	27	49	48	-80	-42	50	-35	20	08
Shape Retention	50	54	33	29	-42	-66	-57	19	-23	-11
Comfort	45	60	-07	-09	-21	-23	-60	37	-13	12
Warmth	28	35	04	-10	-02	-34	-09	19	-32	-31
Perspiration absorption	53	94	52	54	-15	-74	-10	11	82	-63
Cling	-66	-76	-56	-58	38	42	58	-24	64	42

considered. Significant results are circled. The only highly significant correlation is that between perspiration absorption and water imbibition (ASTM
D-2462). Other correlations are of marginal significance. We now have other
wear tests in progress to establish better correlations between the factors
which we feel should be indicative of wearing comfort of garments.

In conclusion, we wish to acknowledge the assistance of Mr. T. A. Odom
and Mr. J. A. Beverly for the statistical evaluations reported.

REFERENCES

Lynn, J. E. *Am. Dyest. Rep.* 61:9 (October 1972).
Scheffe, H. *J. Am. Stat. Assoc.* 47:381-400 (1952).

SECTION IV

INTERACTION OF CLOTHING AND ENVIRONMENT
AND THE VENTILATION OF CLOTHING
FROM BODY MOTION

Chapter 10

THE PSYCHROMETRIC RANGE OF CLOTHING SYSTEMS

Juergen H. Mecheels and Karl H. Umbach

Hohenstein Institutes
Boennigheim, West Germany

THE PSYCHROMETRIC RANGE OF A CLOTHING SYSTEM

An essential function of the human organism is to keep the temperature of his body core constant. Since heat is continually produced within our body at different rates, the heat flow to the environment must be continually adapted to the heat production by means of the body's own temperature-regulating system. As long as a balance is maintained by adaptation of heat loss to heat production, a steady-state of the body's heat content can be kept up. If, however, the heat loss exceeds the heat production (or vice versa), the heat content of the body will decrease (or increase). Such conditions can be maintained only for certain tolerance periods, whereupon a dangerous state of either hypothermia or hyperthermia will be reached.

The body's regulatory system to reduce heat loss is generally known: Firstly, blood flow to the skin and thus heat supply to the external skin surface are reduced by vasoconstriction (which has no greater effect than, for instance, the putting on of a sweater); secondly, there is a decrease of temperature in the extremities (which reduces the heat loss of this part of the body) and, finally, compensatory heat is produced by shivering resulting in an additional energy production of up to 400 watts.

The methods employed by the human regulatory system to increase heat release are much more effective and less stressful to man. Primarily, the steps described above are reversed, *i.e.,* the blood flow to the skin is increased to a maximum, the temperatures of arms and legs are raised to almost core temperature and, finally, evaporative cooling starts; this is by far the most effective temperature-regulating mechanism of our body. Evaporation of one liter of sweat causes a heat loss of about 670 watt · hr.

However ingenious the temperature-regulating system of our body may be, it does not enable us to live naked under the climatic conditions of these latitudes. From his origin, 'homo sapiens' is an inhabitant of the tropics; otherwise nature would have provided him with a coat of fur. So he has to wear clothes instead, and they are an essential part of the regulating system of our body, the best clothing system being that which enables the body's thermoregulation under subjectively felt comfort conditions to control the broadest range of (a) different climatic conditions and (b) different work load (which means different heat production). This range is termed the 'psychrometric range of a clothing system' and will be defined by two limiting temperature values, that is, for any particular clothing system there is a minimum ambient temperature $(T_{a_{min}})$ at which a person with a defined minimum heat production will just not yet feel cold, which means that he can keep his core temperature relatively constant under conditions of subjective comfort. On the other hand, there is a maximum ambient temperature $(T_{a_{max}})$ at which the body/clothing regulatory system will just succeed in keeping the core temperature constant under not quite comfortable but yet bearable conditions even if a higher work load (*i.e.*, heat production) is taken into account.

The difference between $T_{a_{max}}$ and $T_{a_{min}}$ is the psychrometric range of this particular clothing system.

This definition of the psychrometric range is deliberately based on ambient temperatures at which the heat regulating system of the body is able to maintain a steady-state under conditions related to subjective comfort sensations. Thus the minimum and maximum ambient temperatures are illustrative figures for the function of a clothing system in relation to the human temperature regulation, giving some reference points to the clothing designer in expressing the influence of construction details on the psychrometric range of a clothing system. While serving this purpose, it is clearly understood that these limiting values for a particular clothing system are subjected to some psychological influences and are not exactly applicable to all human beings under all conditions.

The energy balance of the human body can be described as:

$$M - P_{ex} = H = H_c + H_e + H_{res} \pm \Delta S \tag{1}$$

The difference between the total metabolic rate M and the external power P_{ex} (*i.e.*, external work per unit time (watt)), is the heat production of the human body H. On the right-hand side of Equation 1 the first terms describe body heat loss, namely, the flux of conductive heat H_c, the flux of evaporative heat H_e and heat release by respiration H_{res}.

The term for H_c comprises radiation, conduction and convection. The impact of radiant heat from the ambient air on clothing will not be discussed in this paper.

Under conditions where energy exchange cannot be balanced, the body's heat content undergoes a change ΔS, while in the steady-state ΔS is 0. As the clothing can influence H_c and H_e only, we get Equation 2

$$H - H_{res} = H_{cl} = H_c + H_e \quad \text{[watt]} \tag{2}$$

where H_{cl} represents the total heat flux from skin to environment, which is transmitted through clothing.

For defining the psychrometric range one has to standardize a minimum ($H_{cl_{min}}$) and a maximum ($H_{cl_{max}}$) heat flux from the body with respect to the rate of heat production according to various physical work levels. Although these figures should be chosen in accord with the intended purpose of a particular clothing system (for instance, in a military uniform they should fit the average duty), two values will be fixed in this paper:

$$H_{cl_{min}} = 80 \text{ watt}$$

$$H_{cl_{max}} = 250 \text{ watt}$$

80 watt heat flux from skin through clothing results from a 105 watt total heat production of a sitting human subject. The difference of approximately 25% is lost by respiration and "insensible perspiration," the latter being effected by water vapor diffusion from the interior of the human body through the skin without activating sweat glands.

If this human subject, who is supposed to be a young, healthy man of about 18-25 years of age, whose body mass is 70 kg with a body height of 173 cm, (in the following he will be cited as "standard man"), is doing medium hard physical work, such as walking on a level black top road at a marching speed of ~4.7 km/hr, he will produce a total heat of 280 watt. As he will sweat sensibly, the "insensible perspiration" is replaced, and in figuring the heat flux through clothing (H_{cl}) the total heat production has only to be adjusted for his respiratory heat loss which, under reasonable ambient climatic conditions, amounts to about 10% of his total heat production, i.e., in this case ~30 watt. Thus the resulting heat flux through clothing is 250 watt.

The thermal properties of a clothing system are determined by its resistance to heat transfer R_c (thermal insulation) and its resistance to moisture transfer R_e, where:

$$R_c = \frac{\overline{T}_s - T_a}{H_c/A} \quad \left[\frac{m^2 \cdot deg}{watt}\right] \tag{3a}$$

$$R_e = \frac{(\overline{P}_s - P_a)}{H_e/A} \quad \left[\frac{m^2 \cdot mmHg}{watt}\right] \tag{3b}$$

$\overline{T}_s - T_a$ is the difference between the mean skin and the ambient temperature. Correspondingly $\overline{P}_s - P_a$ is the difference between the mean water vapor pressure (in mmHg) at the skin and the ambient water vapor pressure. "A" represents the body surface area (in m^2), which can be calculated using the well known DuBois formula (DuBois and DuBois, 1916).

The units of R_c and R_e are related to the often used standard units "clo" and "i_m" (Fourt and Hollies, 1970), namely:

$$1 \text{ clo} = 0.155 \ \frac{m^2 deg}{watt}$$

$$i_m = \frac{\dfrac{R_c \text{ clothing}}{R_e \text{ clothing}}}{\dfrac{R_c \text{ air}}{R_e \text{ air}}} = 0.45 \ \frac{R_c \text{ clothing}}{R_e \text{ clothing}} \tag{4}$$

The coefficient 0.45 will be explained below in connection with Equation 6.

Minimum Ambient Temperature $T_{a_{min}}$

The minimum ambient temperature $T_{a_{min}}$ can now be determined. It is that temperature where the thermoregulating system of the human body is within the cold range; *i.e.,* the mean vapor pressure nearest the skin surface ($\overline{P}_s$) will not appreciably differ from that of the environment; an evaporative heat flux may thus be neglected, and the heat delivery $H_{cl_{min}}$ is given totally as conductive heat (*cf.* Equation 3a). As a result

$$T_{a_{min}} = \overline{T}_s - \frac{H_{cl_{min}} \cdot R_c}{A} \quad \left[^\circ C\right] \tag{5}$$

At the low temperature limit of the comfort range the mean skin temperature is 32°C. Using the 1.83-m^2 body surface area of the above defined "standard man," the following equation is derived from Equation 5:

$$T_{a_{min}} = 32 - \frac{80 \cdot R_c}{1.83} \quad \left[^\circ C\right] \tag{5a}$$

For a normal "business suit," including underwear, the insulation may be assumed as 1.78 clo (according to Gagge *et al.*, 1941). (The suit itself provides 1 clo and the insulation of the surface air layer 0.78 clo.) This is equivalent to $R_c = 0.276$ m^2 · deg/watt.

If this suit is worn by a person sitting quietly, the lowest ambient temperature that will enable him to keep his core temperature constant under comfort conditions is, according to Equation 5a: 19.9°C; the difference from the 21°C temperature, at which the clo unit was defined, derives from using a 32°C $\bar{T}_s$ in place of the 33°C in the original definition.

Maximum Ambient Temperature $T_{a_{max}}$

If the ambient temperature reaches the upper limit of the range where the wearer of a particular clothing system must prevent his core temperature under certain comfort conditions from rising, the body must make use of evaporative cooling. Heat release thus occurs in the form of evaporative as well as conductive heat. The maximum heat production transmitted through clothing $H_{cl_{max}}$ is expressed in Equation 6:

$$H_{cl_{max}} = A \cdot \left[\frac{\bar{T}_s - T_a}{R_c} + \frac{\bar{P}_s - P_a}{R_e} \right] \quad \left[\text{watt} \right] \tag{6}$$

From this the maximum ambient temperature $T_{a_{max}}$ is derived in the following equation:

$$T_{a_{max}} = \bar{T}_s - R_c \left[\frac{H_{cl_{max}}}{.A} - \frac{d \cdot (\bar{P}_s - P_a)}{R_e} \right] \quad \left[°C \right] \tag{7}$$

where d is a "perspiration discomfort factor," which is related to the percentage of sweat wetted skin. The human body would be fully moistened with liquid sweat all over its surface only under extreme conditions; d would then equal 1. This subject, however, would feel extremely uncomfortable in such a way that he could endure this condition only for a very short tolerance period. Therefore, the maximum possible difference of water vapor pressure between skin and ambience is not fully utilized in practice; *i.e.*, d will be smaller than 1. For the calculation of the psychrometric range of a clothing system one can assume d = 0.7. Then, however, the wearer does not feel comfortable but his condition is bearable without affecting his work performance too seriously.

When the human thermoregulating system reaches the upper temperature range, the mean skin temperature rises to 36°C. If we assume $H_{cl_{max}} = 250$ watts as mentioned above, A = 1.83 m^2 and $\bar{P}_s = 44.6$ mmHg (the saturated vapor pressure at 36°C), then Equation 7a results:

$$T_{a_{max}} = 36 - R_c \left[\frac{250}{1.83} - \frac{0.7 \cdot (44.6 - P_a)}{R_e} \right] \quad [^\circ C] \qquad (7a)$$

I In Figure 1 the psychrometric range of the above mentioned "business suit" is shown in a psychrometric chart. $T_{a_{max}}$ is derived from Equation 7a with $R_c = 0.276 \text{ m}^2$ deg/watt and $R_e = 0.245 \text{ m}^2$ mmHg/watt which corresponds to an i_m of 0.5 according to Equation 4.

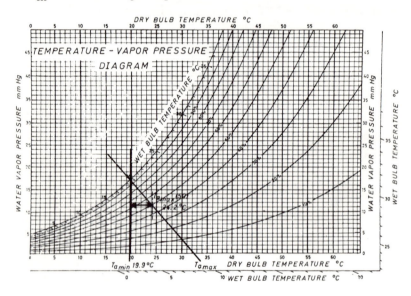

Figure 1. The psychrometric range of a business suit.

The region between the diagram's left- and right-hand straight line is the psychrometric range of this suit.

As it is seen from Equation 7a, $T_{a_{max}}$ depends on the ambient water vapor pressure, or in other words on the ambient relative humidity.

For practical purposes it is desirable to express the psychrometric range of a clothing system by a single figure. Therefore, the upper end of the range is defined as $T_{a_{max}}(50)$, where there exists a relative humidity of 50%. The lower end is given by $T_{a_{min}}$.

In the example of Figure 1 $T_{a_{max}}(50)$ is 24.2°C and, with $T_{a_{min}} = 19.9$°C (*cf.* above), the psychrometric range of this business suit comprises 4.3°C.

The comparatively low value of $T_{a_{max}}(50)$ is not surprising if we consider that the hypothetical "standard man" is doing medium hard work in a business suit.

MEASUREMENT OF THE CHARACTERISTIC
QUANTITIES OF A CLOTHING SYSTEM

In order to calculate the psychrometric range of a particular clothing system we need its resistances to the passage of conductive heat (R_c) and to moisture transfer (R_e).

In Figure 2 these total resistances of a single-layered clothing system are divided into their single resistances: firstly the resistance of the air trapped between skin and textile layer (R_{c_L}', R_{e_L}'), secondly that of the textile layer itself (R_{c_T}, R_{e_T}) and, finally, that of the outer adherent air layer (R_{c_L}'', R_{e_L}'').

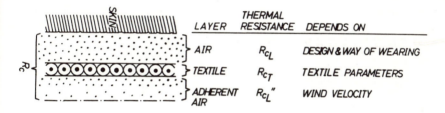

Figure 2. Elements of thermal (R_c) and moisture resistance (R_e) of a single-layer clothing system.

In clothing systems consisting of multiple individual textile layers (the latter in the following marked by an index "i") the resistances of air and textile layers must be summed up.

If textiles only partly cover the body surface, their resistances have to be corrected by an area factor $f_i = a_i/A$, where a_i is the area of the textile layer with number i in relation to the whole body surface area A.

Thus:

$$R_{c_L} = (\sum_i R_{c_{L_i}}') + R_{c_L}'' \quad \text{and} \quad R_{e_L} = (\sum_i R_{e_{L_i}}') + R_{e_L}''$$

$$R_{c_T} = \sum_i R_{c_{T_i}} \cdot f_i \quad \text{and} \quad R_{e_T} = \sum_i R_{e_{T_i}} \cdot f_i$$

In the Hohenstein Institutes, the Multilayer Method has been developed to measure the resistances, $R_{c_{T_i}}$ and $R_{e_{T_i}}$, of individual textile layers employed in a clothing system separately from the resistances of the interjacent and adherent air layers, which are determined by means of the Hohenstein copper manikin, named "Charlie," in connection with the properties of the complete clothing system.

THE MULTILAYER METHOD

Because it is necessary to determine the two related characteristic quantities $R_{c_{T_i}}$ and $R_{e_{T_i}}$ by analogous measurements, the apparatus used has to permit the passage of water vapor as well as the passage of conductive heat through the textile layers. This excludes any two-plate method because of the vapor impermeability of the second plate. A single-plate method, however, is suitable for measuring conductive heat transfer as well as moisture transfer through the textile samples.

In Figure 3 the principle of the Hohenstein Apparatus, which has been described before (Mecheels, 1962; 1968; 1966; 1971a), is shown. A sintered metal plate, 1, which is heated to 35°C and supplied with liquid water, is used. The textile sample, 5, is placed on the plate, while along its outer surface the well-conditioned air of a wind tunnel flows at a defined speed. Care is taken to make sure that no conductive heat and no water vapor can leave the plate except through the sample into the wind tunnel. In order to prevent the wicking of the sample by liquid water from the wet surface of the sintered plate, it is covered with a thin layer of Cellophane which readily transfers water vapor but is impermeable to liquid water. The values of the heat flows, H_c or H_e, result from the power input to the automatically controlled flat plate kept at a constant temperature.

Usually just one single textile layer is placed upon the surface of the plate. But in this setup the amount of heat leaving the sample, and being carried off by the air in the wind tunnel, depends not only on the thermal resistance of the sample itself but also on several other resistances involved in the apparatus. Therefore, the pure textile-layer resistance cannot be obtained. These deficiencies are avoided by the new Multilayer Method. Its main point—from which it got its name—is that not only one, but several layers of the textile

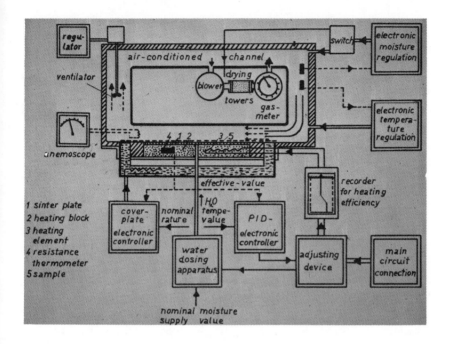

Figure 3. Diagram of the Hohenstein Skin Model.

to be investigated, are placed upon the plate. During several measurements the number of these layers is varied. In order to maintain the same conditions for all sample packages, a standard layer consisting of polyester knitware is placed beneath and on top of them, as shown in Figure 4.

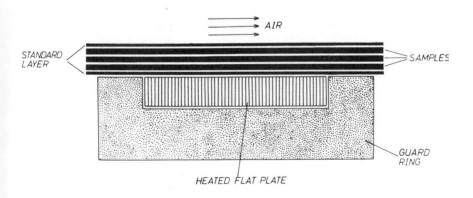

Figure 4. Arrangement of textile layers on flat plate in the Multilayer Method.

If $1/H_c$ is plotted vs the number of sample layers, a straight line is obtained (Figure 5). From its slope, the resistance (R_{cT_i}) of one single layer of the

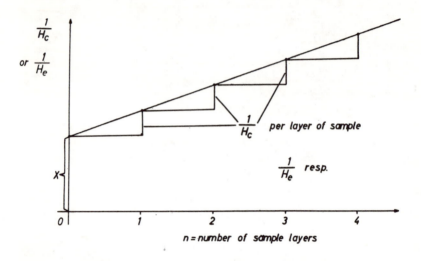

Figure 5. Reciprocal conductive and evaporative heat flux vs number of sample layers.

sample can be deduced, taking into account the temperature difference between plate and air in the wind tunnel as well as the plate's area. In analogy, the corresponding value R_{eT_i} is obtained from the flux of evaporative heat when the plate is supplied with water and thus liberates water vapor. At the intercept of the straight line and the vertical axis, the number of sample layers is zero. **X** represents the sum of all apparatus resistances. Thus the values of R_{cT_i} or R_{eT_i} are entirely independent of any special quality of the apparatus, such as internal resistances, air velocity in the wind tunnel, etc.

Measurements with the Copper
Manikin "Charlie"

The Hohenstein thermoregulative functional model of man (described in Mecheels 1971a; 1971b) is a life-sized copper dummy with flexible limbs. It can be positioned standing, sitting, lying or walking with variable speed. It is electrically heated, where the energy input is either fixed according to the heat production of a particular activity or it is continuously adjusted to maintain a constant body temperature. The manikin is kept in a climatic chamber. It wears the clothing system to be investigated, and thus its total thermal insulation (R_c) is measured, as the power input corresponds to the heat flux (H_c) transmitted through the clothing system. The mean skin temperature

$\overline{T}_s$ of the dummy is obtained from weighted surface temperatures at several points of its body. The total thermal resistance is (*cf.* Equation 3a):

$$R_c = \frac{\overline{T}_s - T_a}{H_c} \cdot A \qquad \left[\frac{m^2 \cdot deg}{watt}\right] \qquad (8)$$

Unfortunately, the manikin cannot supply satisfactory results in analogous measurements of moisture resistance (R_e). Although it is able to simulate the process of perspiration, the desirable reproducibility for a standardized method is lacking. Therefore, R_e is determined in the manner described below, which has been proved to be sufficiently accurate.

The resistance to moisture transfer of a complete clothing system (R_e) equals the sum of the resistances to moisture transfer of all textile layers (R_{e_T}) plus the resistances to moisture transfer of all air layers under, between and above the textiles in the system (R_{e_L}).

$$R_e = R_{e_T} + R_{e_L} = (\sum_i R_{e_T} \cdot f_i) + (\sum_i R_{e_{L_i}}') + R_{e_L}'' \qquad (9)$$

R_{e_T} can be determined by means of the multilayer method described above. R_{e_L}, however, can be elicited from R_{c_L} (*cf.* below), *i.e.*, from the resistance to heat transfer of the air layers within the clothing system and adherent to its outer surface. R_{c_L} is obtained from

$$R_{c_L} = R_c - R_{c_T} \qquad (10)$$

where R_c is determined by means of the copper manikin, R_{c_T} by the multilayer method. As the air layers to be passed are identical for the conductive heat flux as well as the flow of water vapor, the following equations hold:

$$R_{e_L} = \frac{\lambda}{\varphi \cdot D} \cdot R_{c_L} = 0.45 \, R_{c_L} \qquad (11)$$

or

$$R_{e_L} = 0.45 \, (R_c - R_{c_T}) \qquad (11a)$$

where φ = the evaporative heat of water at a skin temperature of $35°C$
       [watt $\cdot$ hr/g$_{water}$];
   λ = the heat conductivity of air in [watt/m deg];
   D = the diffusion coefficient of water vapor in air.

Equations 11 and 11a explain the coefficient 0.45 (units mmHg/deg) already used in Equation 4.

As R_c and R_e of the clothing system are now known, its psychrometric range can be calculated.

THE VENTILATED CLOTHING

The psychrometric range of a clothing system should cover the widest possible variety of work rates (*i.e.*, heat production) of the man wearing it and also various climatic conditions. A man usually adapts his clothing to environmental and work requirements by taking off or putting on pieces of clothing or by opening or closing them. By opening the apertures of his clothes he increases the exchange between the air inside the clothing and the ambient air or, in other words, he allows ventilation. This ventilation is further increased by the pumping effect of the body movements. In the following it will be evaluated quantitatively; taking off and putting on of clothes will not be considered.

The ventilation does not influence the thermal or moisture resistances of the fabrics used (R_{cT_i} and R_{eT_i}), but it changes the properties of the air within the clothing system. These are measured with the copper man "Charlie" mentioned above, who is covered with the clothing system to be investigated. Thus it is possible to determine the heat flux for three different conditions.

Table I. The Effect of Ventilation on a Clothing System

Heat Flux	State of "Charlie"	Ventilation of Clothing
$H_c(1)$	standing	closed
$H_c(2)$	walking at 4.7 km/hr	closed
$H_c(3)$	walking at 4.7 km/hr	open

The difference between the values resulting from the first two lines of this experimental setup shows the effect of the convection forced upon the air trapped within the clothes by walking movements, while there is no exchange of air with the environment.

This change of total thermal resistance of the clothing system, however, is not very large, whereas the exchange of air through opened apertures of the suit, influenced by walking movements according to line 3 of the table above, significantly reduces the thermal resistance.

It should be noted that the rate of ventilation not only depends on the walking movements but also on the fitting of the clothes, with a better ventilation for loose-fitting than for tight-fitting ones.

Regarding Equations 5 and 7 for $T_{a_{min}}$ and $T_{a_{max}}$, respectively, for the psychrometric range, it has to be decided which of the three conditions of the table above is to be considered.

As it would make no sense to define a lower temperature limit under conditions of maximum ventilation, because the wearer of the suit would close his apertures as soon as he feels cold, $T_{a_{min}}$ is calculated with values resulting from the first state indicated in Table I. Moreover, the heat flux for $T_{a_{min}}$ is fixed for a sitting person, thus eliminating body movements.

Therefore, the third state indicated in Table I is of interest only for the calculation of the maximum ambient temperature $T_{a_{max}}$, where the wearer of the suit is performing medium hard work, thus being interested in as much ventilation as possible. Since ventilation represents a bypass for heat and moisture which do not have to pass through the textiles, Equation 6 must be modified accordingly

The effect of ventilation can be expressed in terms of resistance to heat transfer (R_{c_v}) and of resistance to moisture transfer (R_{e_v}), both these values growing smaller as ventilation increases. Without ventilation these two resistances will be infinite. As they are shunted in parallel with the above considered, "normal," resistances of the clothing system, the reciprocal values of all these resistances corresponding to the conductivities must be added in order to obtain the total resistance of the clothes including ventilation:

i.e.,
$$\frac{1}{R_c(3)} = \frac{1}{R_c(2)} + \frac{1}{R_{c_v}} \tag{12}$$

and
$$\frac{1}{R_e(3)} = \frac{1}{R_e(2)} + \frac{1}{R_{e_v}} \tag{12a}$$

where $R_c(2)$ and $R_c(3)$ are calculated according to Equation 8 from the table's $H_c(2)$ and $H_c(3)$ as measured with copperman "Charlie." Thus R_{c_v} is derived from the difference between $H_c(3)$ and $H_c(2)$. $R_e(2)$ can be calculated from $R_c(2)$ by Equations 9 through 11a, using the values of the textiles alone obtained by the Multilayer Method, as described earlier. Because the ventilating air carrying off thermal heat and water vapor is identical, R_{e_v} can be obtained from R_{c_v}, namely:

$$R_{e_v} = R_{c_v} \cdot \frac{c_p \cdot \zeta}{\varphi} = \frac{0.279 \cdot 1.146}{0.63} \cdot R_{c_v} = 0.508 \cdot R_{c_v} \left[\frac{m^2 mmHg}{watt} \right] \tag{13}$$

where c_p = the specific heat of air in [watt $\cdot$ hr/kg $\cdot$ deg],

ζ = its density at 35°C under normal pressure in [kg/m^3], and

φ = the evaporative heat of water at 35°C in [watt $\cdot$ hr/mmHg $\cdot$ m^3].

Thus $R_e(3)$ can be calculated according to Equation 12a.

If the resistances in Equation 6 are linked to the third state in Table I as explained above, this equation changes to:

$$H_{cl_{max}} = A \cdot \left[\frac{\overline{T}_s - T_a}{R_c(3)} + (\overline{P}_s - P_a) \cdot (\frac{1}{R_e(2)} + \frac{1}{R_{e_v}}) \right] \quad [\text{watt}] \quad (14)$$

Thus the maximum ambient temperature $T_{a_{max}}$ for ventilated clothing is given by the following Equation 14a:

$$T_{a_{max}} = \overline{T}_s - R_c(3) \left[\frac{H_{cl_{max}}}{A} - d \cdot (\overline{P}_s - P_a) \cdot (\frac{1}{R_e(2)} + \frac{1}{R_{e_v}}) \right] \quad [^\circ C] \quad (14a)$$

where
$\overline{T}_s$ = 36°C,

$\overline{P}_s$ = 44.6 mmHg

$H_{cl_{max}}$ = 250 watts

A = 1.83 m^2

d = 0.7

As explained previously in this chapter, Equation 14b is obtained finally:

$$T_{a_{max}} = 36 - R_c(3) \left[136.6 - 0.7 \cdot (44.6 - P_a) \cdot \frac{1}{R_e(2)} + \frac{1}{R_{e_v}}) \right] \quad [^\circ C] . \quad (14b)$$

QUANTITATIVE RESULTS

In order to demonstrate the applicability of the derived formulas, as well as the quantitative relations between construction details of fabric or clothing design and the resulting psychrometric range, its limiting temperatures shall be examined for a particular clothing system.

As part of a research contract, the Hohenstein Institutes have developed a new specially ventilated fatigue uniform. The demands to be fulfilled by this system were: ample liberty to movement and a regulating ventilation system, that allows adaptability of the body/clothing temperature regulatory system to the widest possible range of ambient climatic conditions or work rates, respectively. The design of this fatigue dress is shown in Figure 6. It has a one-piece front (Figure 6A), while its back piece consists of two parts, of which the top one can either be worn inside the waistband (Figure 6B) or outside for better ventilation (Figure 6C). The waistband itself may be loose because the trousers are kept in position by the one-piece front. Beside several adjustable apertures for ventilation at the cuffs of sleeves and trouser legs and at the chest, the suit has zippered slits under the armpits (Figure 6D).

For maximal thermal insulation the dress is worn with all its apertures closed; by opening them one by one the system can be adapted to higher temperatures or heavier work.

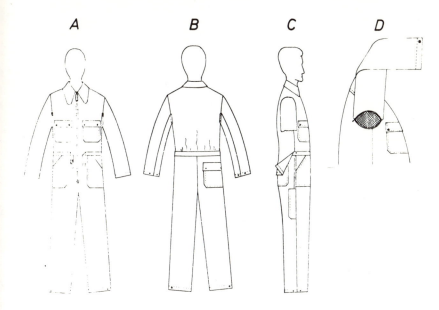

Figure 6. Diagram of the Hohenstein fatigue dress.

Table II contains the characteristic quantities measured with this fatigue dress, covering the entire manikin's body, worn over a set of cotton underwear and a cotton shirt. The clothing system thus consists of two and, at the body's upper part, three textile layers. The values show the influence of all parameters effecting the maximum and, as far as reasonable, the minimum ambient temperatures that can be tolerated by the wearer of the suit in a steady-state under subjective comfort conditions, as explained in the first section of this chapter.

Line 1 of Table II contains the data for the fatigue dress without ventilation and without forced convection, *i.e.*, with the copper manikin "Charlie" standing quietly. $T_{a_{min}}$ amounts to 20.0°C, $T_{a_{max}}$ to 26.1°C according to Equations 5a and 7a, respectively; the latter value is not reasonable because a person doing medium hard work (and $T_{a_{max}}$ is based on a heat flux H_{cl} of 250 watts) will always move and is likely to open the ventilation apertures of his clothing in order to feel more comfortable.

Line 2 describes a forced convection of the internal air; the copper manikin is walking. However, any exchange of air through the outermost textile layer of the clothing as well as any ventilation is prevented. Under such conditions a statement of $T_{a_{max}}$ seems more reasonable, whereas now $T_{a_{min}}$ should be stated in a resting position as in Line 1. As mentioned before, the forced convection has no essential effect on the values obtained.

Table II. Quantitative Results Applying the Prognostic Formulas to the Hohenstein Fatigue Dress

Line	Forced Convec-	Venti-lation (m³/hr)	Fabric	R_c Cloth-ing System Charlie	R_{cTu} Under-wear Plate	R_{cTo} Over-Garment Plate	R_{cT} Textile Layers $R_{cTu} + R_{cTo}$	R_{cL} Air-Layers $R_c - R_{cT}$	R_{cv} Venti-lation Charlie	R_{eL} Air-Layers from R_{cL}(11)	R_{eT} Textile Layers Plate	R_e Cloth-ing System Eq.9, 12a	R_{ev} Venti-lation from R_{cv}(13)	T_{amin} T_{amax} a = 50% rH
							$m^2 \cdot$ deg/watt					$m^2 \cdot$ mmHg/watt		°C
1	–	–	normal	0.275	0.058	0.0258	0.0838	0.191	without	0.086	0.136	0.222	without	20.0 (26.1)
2	+	–	normal	0.247	0.058	0.0258	0.0838	0.163	without	0.0734	0.136	0.209	without	(21.2) 27.6
3	–	–	light	0.262	0.058	0.0129	0.0709	0.191	without	0.086	0.113	0.199	without	20.5 (28.1)
4	+	–	light	0.234	0.058	0.0129	0.0709	0.163	without	0.0734	0.113	0.186	without	(21.8) 29.6
5	+	1.0	normal	0.235	0.058	0.0258	0.0838	0.163	4.795	0.0734	0.136	0.192	2.436	29.1
6	+	2.4	normal	0.220	0.058	0.0258	0.0838	0.163	2.013	0.0734	0.136	0.174	1.023	30.8
7	+	5	normal	0.196	0.058	0.0258	0.0838	0.163	0.959	0.0734	0.136	0.146	0.487	33.2
8	+	1.0	light	0.223	0.058	0.0129	0.0709	0.163	4.795	0.0734	0.113	0.173	2.436	30.8
9	+	1.0	normal imper-meable	0.241	0.058	0.033	0.091	0.163	4.795	0.0734		2.436	2.436	5.9
10	+	2.4	normal imper-meable	0.225	0.058	0.033	0.091	0.163	1.998	0.0734		1.015	1.015	11.4
11	+	2.4	normal imper-meable (H_{cl}=180 W)	0.225	0.058	0.033	0.091	0.163	1.998	0.0734		1.015	1.015	19.5
12	+	2.4	normal imper-meable (H_{cl}=180 W)	0.225	0.058	0.033	0.091	0.163	1.998	0.0734		1.015	1.015	(φ_a = 95% rh)

The influence of the thermal insulation of the overgarment's fabric on the insulation of the entire clothing system is shown by replacing the "normal" material of this fatigue dress by a "light" material with only half the thermal insulation and also half the moisture resistance to maintain the same i_m. Then $T_{a_{min}}$ in Line 3 and $T_{a_{max}}$ in Line 4 differ only slightly from the corresponding values in Lines 1 and 2; the total R_c and R_e values of the clothing are not altered, essentially, even by such a large change in material. Ignorance of this fact often leads to false estimates by the textile industry.

If we open all the ventilation apertures of the dress and also allow a certain exchange between air trapped within the clothing and the ambient air through the outermost textile layers, the flux of conductive heat from our copper manikin increases by 20% as compared with Line 1 and by 11% as compared with Line 2. This means that H_{c_v} is nearly 9 times smaller than H_c in Line 2. In spite of this, there is a considerable rise in the maximum tolerable ambient temperature in Line 6 as compared with Line 2, up to $T_{a_{max}} = 30.8°C$. From R_{c_v} we can calculate by means of the specific heat of air that about 2.4 m^3/hr of air must have been exchanged between clothing and environment. The fatigue dress had to be rather tight-fitting to comply with safety prescriptions for working clothes. H_{c_v} could be further increased by the better ventilation provided by looser fitting clothes. The effect on $T_{a_{max}}$ is calculated in Line 5 on the basis of an air passage of only 1.0 m^3/hr. The effect of ventilation on the maximum temperature thus decreases.

In a ventilated clothing system, the influence of the thermal insulation of the outermost textile layer is rather limited. In Line 8 the "light" material from Line 4 is used again, with only slight passage of air. There is obviously no great difference in $T_{a_{max}}$ as compared with Line 5.

Finally, let us study a clothing system which has an outermost layer that is completely impermeable to water vapor, such as is used for rainwear, for NBC protective clothing and for certain work clothes. The thermal resistance of this fabric will be larger than the resistance of the fabrics used in Lines 1 through 8. Therefore, in Line 9 $R_{c_{T_0}}$ is assumed to be 0.033 m^2 deg/watt. In this clothing system the whole transport of moisture is left to ventilation. It can be seen that, with minimal ventilation, this task is too much for the working dress studied here; a man doing average work can not reach the steady-state except in a cold environment near the freezing point. Even with ventilation of 2.4 m^3/hr of the fatigue dress, according to Line 4, the maximum comfort temperature will reach only 11.4°C (*cf*. Line 10). The wearer is simply not able to do medium hard work with this clothing. However, if in Line 11 we replace $H_{cl_{max}}$ by a heat flux of $H_{cl} = 180$ watts instead of 250 watts, in other words, if the wearer of the dress performs only light work, then we reach acceptable temperature ranges. Therefore, only light work will be possible in such impermeable clothing. But a minimum air exchange of

2.4 m^3/hr is required; a few ventilation eyelets in a raincoat will never be adequate for this.

The problem with rainwear is the high relative humidity, with the ambient air at nearly 100%. Therefore, in Line 12 a $T_{a_{max}}$ of 18.5°C results if the relative humidity is assumed to be 95%.

CONCLUSION

It can be stated in summary that with the Multilayer Method the characteristic (inherent) resistance values of textiles can be measured. These values enter additively into the total resistances of a clothing system in which the textiles are applied. With the copper manikin "Charlie" the total thermal resistances can be obtained, and how they are influenced by ventilation can be determined. By inserting all quantities into the derived formulas, a minimum and a maximum tolerable ambient temperature, $T_{a_{min}}$ and $T_{a_{max}}$, respectively, are calculated as the limits of the psychrometric range of a clothing system. One can estimate how this range is influenced by construction details.

In this chapter the influence of air velocity outside the clothing has not been mentioned. It is possible, however, to determine the insulation of the outer adherent air layer in accord with wind velocity according to the data of Herrington and Gagge (Winslow *et al.*, 1940). Moreover, a strong wind will force some air at least out of the outermost textile layer, thus altering its inherent resistance to conductive heat and moisture transfer in analogy to the influence of ventilation on the total resistances of the whole clothing system.

Investigations of these problems are presently done, as well as the testing of these prognostic formulas, by controlled climatic chamber tests with human subjects. A particular interest lies in the relation between the defined discomfort factor, d, and the subjective comfort rate.

The predictive calculations in this paper do not give any information about the tolerance time during which a clothing system can be worn outside its psychrometric range. But the measured quantities can easily be adapted to formulas published by Goldman and Givoni (1972; 1973a; 1973b) to answer this question.

The psychrometric range alone, with its minimum and maximum temperature, however, is found to be very useful to textile and garment designers.

In this chapter we gave a brief survey of the measurements and interpretation of characteristic garment and textile thermal data. The psychrometric range of a clothing system has been redefined. So far $T_{a_{max}}$ had been calculated for entirely wetted skin; it was thus defined as maximum ambient temperature for physical thermal balance. Now we have introduced the discomfort factor, d, and $T_{a_{max}}$ is altered to the maximum ambient temperature of bearable subjective discomfort.

To evaluate the textile data a new multilayer method on a perspiring flat plate was presented and, finally, a copper manikin with flexible limbs allowed determination of the garment's thermal resistances under different states, reflecting the fact that the thermal insulation of clothing is not a constant value. The method described allows quantitative statements as to the ventilation of clothing.

REFERENCES

DuBois, D. and E. F. DuBois. "A Formula to Estimate the Approximate Surface Area if Height and Weight be Known," *Arch. Int. Med.* 17:863 (1916).

Fourt, L. and N. R. S. Hollies. *Clothing: Comfort and Function* (New York: Marcel Dekker, 1970).

Gagge, A. P., A. C. Burton and H. C. Bazett. *Science* 94:428 (1941).

Givoni, B. and R. F. Goldman. "Predicting Rectal Temperature Response to Work, Environment, and Clothing," *J. Appl. Physiol.* 32:812 (1972).

Givoni, B. and R. F. Goldman. "Predicting Heart Rate Response to Work, Environment, and Clothing," *J. Appl. Physiol.* 34:201 (1973a).

Givoni, B. and R. F. Goldman. "Predicting Effects of Heat Acclimatization on Heart Rate and Rectal Temperature," *J. Appl. Physiol.* 35:875 (1973b).

Mecheels, J. *Melliand Textilber* 43:585 (1962).

Mecheels, J. *Textilveredlung* 3:513 (1968).

Mecheels, J. H., R. M. Demeler and E. Kachel. *Textile Res. J.* 36:375 (1966).

Mecheels, J. *Melliand Textilber* 52:843, 967, 1215 (1971a).

Mecheels, J. "Concomitant Heat and Moisture Transmission Properties of Clothing," *3rd Shirley International Seminar* (June 15-17, 1971b).

Winslow, C. E. A., A. P. Gagge and L. P. Herrington. *Amer. J. Physiol.* 131:79 (1940).

Chapter 11

EFFECTS OF BODY MOTION ON CONVECTIVE AND EVAPORATIVE HEAT EXCHANGES THROUGH VARIOUS DESIGNS OF CLOTHING

John R. Breckenridge

U. S. Army Research Institute of Environmental Medicine
Natick, Massachusetts 01760

It has long been recognized that body motion, by setting up convection currents at the surface and within a clothing ensemble, increases heat exchange between the wearer and his environment. Such currents not only accelerate the rate of convective heat transfer but also the rate of evaporative cooling for the sweating man since this also depends on air motion. Belding *et al.* (1947), from studies on two subjects at the Harvard Fatigue Laboratory, reported in 1946 that the intrinsic insulation value of an Arctic uniform was reduced from 2.7 clo with the subjects standing, to 1.3 clo for level walking at 6.4 km/hr (4 mph). He explained this 50% reduction by considering separately the contributions of the fabrics and of the air spaces between layers. He calculated from their thicknesses that the fabrics provided 1.7 clo, and the air spaces 1.4 clo in still air (a slightly high total of 3.1 clo). During activity, he reasoned, the insulation of the air spaces could fall to less than 0.5 clo, a drop of 0.9 clo; the effect of air motion within the fabrics could not be estimated but apparently accounted for the remainder of the insulation decrease (0.5 clo).

Little additional work to quantify the effects of body motion for other types of clothing was conducted until recently, when the need for such data became essential to the success of modeling techniques for predicting environmental stress and tolerance for active men (Givoni and Goldman, 1972).

FACTORS DETERMINING HEAT REMOVAL
BY AIR MOVEMENT IN CLOTHING

Past studies on changes in clothing insulation in wind (Breckenridge and Woodcock, 1950) show that the loss in insulation value at a given wind speed is largely dependent on such ensemble design parameters as thickness and number of windbreak layers, fit and drape of the garments, fiber density, flexibility of layers, and adequacy of closures. These factors, which affect the air exchange with the outside as well as resistance to air circulation within the clothing, are essentially the same ones which control the effects of clothing "pumping" during body motion. The mechanisms of energy exchange are not identical for the two cases, but it is obvious that no one equation will adequately describe the changes in heat and vapor transfer with body motion for all types of clothing. It is possible, however, that a *single form of equation,* in which only the coefficients and exponents are changed to reflect design effects, will ultimately prove to be satisfactory.

Some insight into the various factors which determine the resistance to air movement through and between clothing layers is provided by Fonseca's analysis of results from two wind studies on cylinders covered with multiple spaced fabric sleeves (Fonseca and Breckenridge, 1965a; 1965b).

The first study employed three, equally spaced layers of blanket cloth supported on a 7.6-cm (3-in.) diameter cylinder by bakelite rings, as shown in Figure 1. Holes drilled in the bottom rings allowed air to enter from the

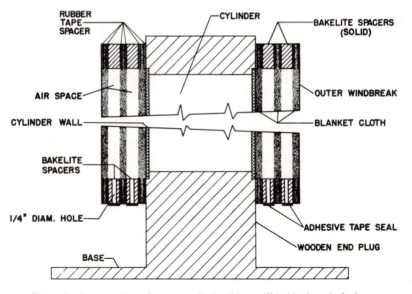

Figure 1. Cross-section of copper cylinder "dressed" in blanket cloth sleeves.

outside ("open closures"), except when covered with tape ("sealed closures"). An impermeable outer cover was used in some experiments. Results for layer spacings from 0.32 to 1.91 cm (0.125 in. to 0.75 in.) are shown in Figure 2.

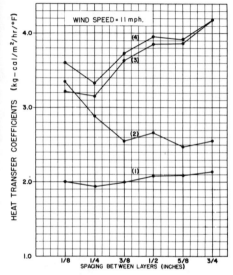

(1) SEALED CLOSURES, IMPERMEABLE OUTER WINDBREAK.
(2) SEALED CLOSURES, NO OUTER WINDBREAK.
(3) OPEN CLOSURES, IMPERMEABLE OUTER WINDBREAK.
(4) OPEN CLOSURES, NO OUTER WINDBREAK.

Figure 2. Results of study of wind penetration through three spaced blanket cloth sleeves. Details of experimental apparatus are shown in Figure 1.

With sealed closures and no windbreak (curve 2), larger spacings resulted in lower heat loss. Apparently the resistance to air flow through large spaces is sufficiently low that most of the air which penetrates the system is diverted by the middle layer and forced to flow through the outer space. This occurred even though the blanket cloth was not particularly wind-resistant. However, at spacings of 0.64 cm (0.25 in.) or less, the resistance to air flow in the outer space is high enough to reduce this shunting action; i.e., the resistances of the air space and middle layer were more evenly matched. More air was forced into the hot inner space, causing a sharp rise in heat loss. Evidence that a narrow space provided high resistance is also inferred from curves 3 and 4, for open closures. At 0.32-cm (0.125-in.) spacing, air entering the inner space via the closures only (curve 3, with outer windbreak) had about the same effect as layer penetration with no windbreak (curve 2). This indicates that the air space resistance was limiting the amount of air entering the openings to about the same level as that which passed through the middle layer with the closures sealed. This limiting of closure penetration rapidly decreased at larger spacings. In fact, at 0.95-cm (0.375 in.) and larger spacing, a windbreak layer had little effect on heat loss (curve 4 vs curve 3), suggesting that all the heat loss was caused by closure penetration. This seems reasonable in view of the earlier discussion regarding shunting of air around the middle layer when spacing is large.

In actual clothing, the path lengths for air flow between layers would usually be much longer than on the cylinder. Accordingly, resistance to such flow would be much higher, making it less likely that a unidirectional motion through an air space would be set up by wind or by pumping during body motion. Since body motion produces relatively weak pressures for moving air, it seems more reasonable to expect that increases in heat loss and evaporative transfer are caused more by increased random air motion within the clothing than by increased infiltration or air exchange with the external environment. This would be particularly true where the layers are flexible and well defined air spaces do not exist.

The second study, using a 15.2-cm (6-in.) copper and plastic cylinder which allowed measurement of local heat transfer coefficients, also used spaced, 3-layer systems (1.27 cm fixed spacing), but employed less permeable layers (a windbreak fabric); measurements were made with empty air spaces, and with one or both spaces filled with a pile material. Results, shown in Figure 3, support the conclusions of the blanket cloth study. Only those for the windward position (0°) will be discussed here. With no filling material in either space (curve 1), the coefficient is somewhat higher than for a system with an impermeable middle layer (curve 3), but much lower than for systems with filling material in the outer space (curves 4 and 5), which limited shunting of air around the middle layer. Potential for penetration of this layer was then quite high, particularly when the inner space was unfilled and thus offered little resistance to flow. The coefficient for this combination (Fonseca and Breckenridge, 1965) is over twice that with both spaces empty (Belding *et al.*, 1947). The reverse condition exists in a system (Breckenridge and Goldman, 1976) in which an empty outer space (low shunting resistance) was combined with a filled inner space (high resistance behind the middle layer). Here the coefficient is only slightly higher than for a system with an impermeable middle layer (Breckenridge and Woodcock, 1950).

THE PHYSICAL-PHYSIOLOGICAL APPROACH TO MEASUREMENT OF CLOTHING HEAT TRANSFER

The Military Ergonomics Division at USARIEM routinely evaluates experimental and standard military clothing ensembles on a standing, life-size, electrically heated copper manikin, (Breckenridge and Goldman, 1976; Goldman, 1967; Goldman and Breckenridge, 1970), dressed in a fatigue

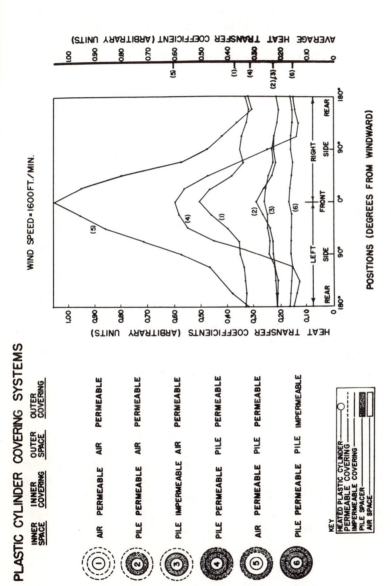

Figure 3. Local heat transfer coefficients for various combinations of filled and empty air spaces.

uniform. Insulation values, including boundary air layer, are measured with the system dry, at 0.3 m/s air movement. The evaporative potential, as given by Woodcock's moisture permeability index i_m (1962) is also determined. For this, the formfitting cotton "skin" which covers the manikin is completely wetted and the power input required to maintain constant manikin temperature measured. The two parameters are calculated using the equation:

$$H_D = \frac{6.46 \, (T_s - T_{ad}) \, A_s}{clo_T} \tag{1}$$

and

$$H_W = \frac{6.46 \, A_s}{clo_T} \left[(T_{sw} - T_a) + 2.2 \, i_m \, (P_{sw} - \emptyset_a \, P_a) \right] \tag{2}$$

where
H_D = power input with the cotton "skin" dry, W
H_W = power input with the cotton "skin" wet, W
A_s = manikin surface area, m^2
T_s = average manikin surface temperature, dry, $^\circ C$
T_{sw} = average manikin surface temperature, with wetted "skin," $^\circ C$
T_{ad} = ambient air temperature, dry run, $^\circ C$
T_a = ambient air temperature, wet run, $^\circ C$
P_{sw} = saturated vapor pressure at T_{sw}, mmHg
P_a = saturated vapor pressure at T_a, mmHg
$\emptyset_a$ = ambient air relative humidity, percent
clo_T = total insulation of clothing plus boundary air layer, clo units (Gagge et al., 1941)
i_m = moisture permeability index, dimensionless.

The factor 2.2 is the ratio of the evaporative to convective coefficients of heat exchange, calculated from the modified Lewis Relation (Nishi and Gagge, 1974) for air at normal barometric pressure, in $^\circ C/mmHg$. It essentially converts the vapor pressure difference ($P_{sw} - \emptyset_a \, P_a$) to an equivalent temperature difference. The last part of the second equation (wet "skin") is the maximal evaporative capacity of the environment (E_{max}) for the ensemble and environment involved, i.e.:

$$E_{max} = 6.46 \, A_s \, (i_m/clo_T) \, (2.2) \, (P_{sw} - \emptyset_a \, P_a) \tag{3}$$

where E_{max} is in W. It will be seen that the evaporative coefficient is given by the ratio i_m/clo_T for the ensemble.

Results from measurements on the static manikin are valid for showing effects of design modifications of similarly constructed ensembles, *i.e.*, those with similar fit, drape, number of layers, closures, etc. They probably are less reliable for comparing dynamic ensemble characteristics, when design differences which might have an important effect on "pumping" coefficients are involved. Where these differences exist, or are suspected, the manikin evaluations have usually been validated in climatic chamber calorimetry studies utilizing human volunteers. This practice will have to be continued until sufficient correlations between design characteristics and "pumping" coefficients become available, to allow realistic estimates of dynamic insulating and evaporative parameters from copper manikin values for any type of clothing.

A typical example of an instance where it was felt necessary to conduct chamber validations following manikin measurements was a study (Breckenridge and Goldman, 1976) to assess the effects of venting raincoats across the shoulders, to promote air circulation and evaporative cooling. Two styles of raincoats, one of cotton with water repellent treatment (which allowed substantial vapor transfer) and another with an impermeable plastic coating, respectively with and without vents, were measured over fatigues on the manikin. To demonstrate the effect of the vents, measurements were made with the raincoats stationary, and while being "pumped" once per second using a flapping device. Drawstrings connected to a rotating arm were attached to the edges of the shoulder flap and tension adjusted so that, with the flap pulled open, the fabric over the shoulders, arms and chest was pulled toward the rear. Despite this motion, which also caused the bottom of the raincoat to sway, the vents produced less than 5% change in clo_T or i_m; in fact, the values were not appreciably different from those obtained on the static system ($clo_T = 1.7$; $i_m/clo_T = 0.14$). These results, particularly the failure to demonstrate an effect of motion, were entirely contrary to expectations and clearly required further investigation using human subjects. A chamber study was therefore conducted in which the change of stored body heat (ΔS) with time, was determined on subjects wearing the various rainwear items while going through a standard rest-walk-rest routine. Rate of heat storage ($\Delta S/hr$) was determined from measurements of skin and rectal temperatures on the subjects as they sat, or walked on a treadmill at 3.5 mph.

The results of the chamber study are shown in Figure 4. Clo_T and i_m/clo_T values from the manikin study, plus results on a poncho, are shown to the right. In comparing trends in ΔS during the walking period, one observes that no effect of the vent in promoting increased cooling is evident with the standard raincoat. In fact, the average rate of storage seems higher with a vent, both for the first 30 min of walking and for the final 20 min, when

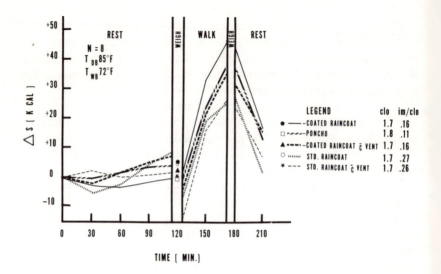

Figure 4. Results of physiological study of heat storage in 4 raincoats and poncho during a rest-walk-rest routine. Standard fatigue uniform was worn under rainwear items.

the rises with and without vents both became less abrupt. Both of these rain-coats probably allowed sufficient evaporative cooling to delay the need for heavy sweating (and more cooling) until 30 min into the walk, when ΔS was about 15 kcal; body temperature rise was then only about 0.3°C (0.5°F). With the impermeable plastic raincoats, which had much lower i_m/clo_T values and allowed less evaporative cooling per se, the effect of the vent in minimizing ΔS is apparent, especially during the first 30 min (about 25 kcal with vent vs 30 kcal without vent). This is not a large difference, probably because the subjects were only moderately stressed and not sweating maximally, but does indicate some enhancement of air circulation by the vent in an impermeable garment.

The most noteworthy curve is that for the poncho. This curve closely parallels that for the coated raincoat with vent, although the manikin i_m/clo_T for the poncho is only 0.11 vs 0.16 for the raincoat. When wearing the poncho, large folds of impermeable fabric hang down loosely over the arms and trunk. These folds are raised and lowered by the movement of the arms during walking, causing rapid influx of ambient air, which moves freely across the arms and trunk and greatly increases evaporative cooling. The raincoat, on the other hand, is much more form-fitting, especially around the arms and upper trunk, and offers much higher resistance to free air circulation. This is an example of a difference in design characteristics which is not correctly assessed by the manikin.

Conclusions regarding the effectiveness of a vent, based on manikin results, are far less in error owing to the design similarities of the two raincoats involved in each comparison (*i.e.*, with and without vent). Of course, the quantitative prediction of stress from manikin data might be considerably in error, depending on the amount by which body motion changed clo_T and i_m/clo_T.

EMPIRICAL EXPRESSIONS FOR DESCRIBING EFFECTS OF BODY MOTION

At USARIEM, a program to determine the effects of body motion on clo_T and i_m/clo_T for various types of clothing was initiated in 1972, in connection with the development of a mathematical model for predicting the time course of change in rectal temperature in man as a function of activity level, environment, etc. (Givoni and Goldman, 1972). This model, which has since been expanded to predict heart rate and skin temperature changes, is invaluable for estimating environmental stress on the active man, and his tolerance under extreme conditions. Its success requires an accurate assessment of heat exchange with the environment, and therefore a correct description of the effective clo_T and i_m/clo_T for any activity level in the clothing and equipment being worn.

Initial studies were conducted on walking subjects wearing shorts, standard fatigue uniform (STD), or chemical protective overgarments over fatigue (STD + OG). Based on the final rectal temperatures, it was apparent that evaporative loss was underestimated using standard manikin values of i_m/clo_T; with the STD and (STD + OG) uniforms, errors were quite large at low air speed (0.5 m/s) but much less serious at 5 m/s. These discrepancies were resolved by introducing the concept of an effective wind velocity (V_{eff}) which combined the effects of external air motion and body motion. The expression which produced the best fit to the data at both 0.5 m/s and 5 m/s was:

$$V_{eff} = V_{air} + 0.004 \ (M-105) \tag{4}$$

where V_{air} = net air velocity, m/s and
          M = metabolic heat production of subject, W.

The term (M-105) is simply the elevation of metabolic production above the normal resting 105 watt level. For treadmill walking, as in these experiments, V_{air} is simply the ambient windspeed; if the subjects had been progressing forward, V_{air} would be the algebraic sum of walking speed plus air velocity, *i.e.*, less than windspeed for walking with the wind, greater for walking into the wind. Essentially, V_{eff} may be considered as a means of adjusting clo_T

and i_m/clo_T manikin values measured at the standard 0.3 m/s air motion in our chamber, to those which would be measured in a wind equal to V_{eff}. This is illustrated using the curves for a tropical fatigue uniform shown in Figure 5. If the subject's activity is such that total heat production (M) is

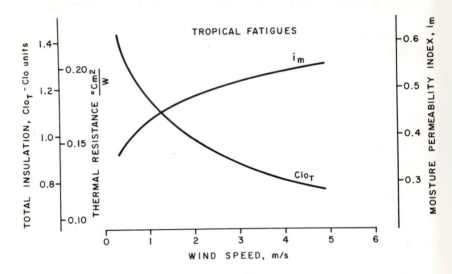

Figure 5. Variation of clo_T and i_m with wind speed for a tropical fatigue uniform.

470 W, the equivalent increase in wind velocity is about 1.5 m/s. Thus, V_{eff} adjusts the manikin values, which are routinely measured at 0.3 m/s to new values for 1.5 + 0.3, or 1.8 m/s. In the case of the fatigues, this lowers the clo_T value from 1.43 to about 1.02 clo, and increases i_m from 0.37 to 0.48; i_m/clo_T increases from 0.26 to 0.47, which almost doubles the predicted maximal evaporative heat loss.

The derivation of equations relating actual clo_T and i_m/clo_T values for the ensembles to activity has been accomplished by empirical fit, using cooling data from this and other studies in various environments for wide range of activity levels (walking speeds). The coefficients in these equations were adjusted to produce the best agreement between final measured and predicted rectal temperatures (T_{ref}). The predicted value for T_{ref} was calculated using the formula:

$$T_{ref} = 36.75 + 0.004 \ (M - W_{ex}) + (0.025/clo_T) \ (T_a - 36) \tag{5}$$
$$+ \ 0.8e \exp 0.0047 \ (E_{req} - E_{max})$$

where W_{ex} = external work performed, W

E_{req} = required evaporative cooling, equal to the sum of metabolic
and sensible heat gain from the environment, W.

The results of these manipulations produced the following relationships:

Clothing	clo_T	i_m/clo_T
Shorts	$0.57\ V_{eff}^{-0.30}$	$1.20\ V_{eff}^{+0.30}$
Shorts and short-sleeve shirt	$0.74\ V_{eff}^{-0.28}$	$0.94\ V_{eff}^{+0.28}$
STD fatigues	$0.99\ V_{eff}^{-0.25}$	$0.75\ V_{eff}^{+0.25}$
STD + OG *	$1.50\ V_{eff}^{-0.15}$	$0.51\ V_{eff}^{+0.15}$

With still heavier clothing systems the V_{eff} exponent continues to decrease, approaching 0.05 for an Arctic uniform, while for STD fatigues plus body armor the exponent 0.20 appears to provide a reasonable fit to the experimental data (Haisman and Goldman, 1974). It is interesting to note that the clo_T curve for STD fatigues from the above equation is almost exactly superimposed on the curve for wind (Figure 5) if the coefficient 0.99 is increased to 1.16. The reason for such a shift in coefficients is not readily apparent. However, it would be fortunate if the equations, with such minor modifications, were found to describe the clo_T and i_m/clo_T curves for the other uniforms. This would imply that manikin measurements could be used to derive the equation coefficients and exponents of V_{eff}. It would also make the equations correct for the resting as well as the active man. Whether or not prediction of the activity curves in this manner is possible for other types, weights and designs of clothing is at present a matter for conjecture. It hardly seems likely, however, that the effects of wind and body motion will always be identical, as the above suggests, in view of the many combinations of fit, drape, layer stiffness, fabric permeability, etc., which are possible.

OTHER APPROACHES IN THE ASSESSMENT OF BODY MOTION EFFECTS

Interest in the problem of assessing the effects of body motion on heat exchange has stimulated additional work at USARIEM and other laboratories. A novel method for measuring both local and overall coefficients during exercise has recently been described by Nishi *et al.* (1975), at the John B. Pierce

---

*A previously published value of 0.20 for the coefficient for this ensemble represents a typographic error in translating from the graph (published simultaneously) which portrays the correct 0.15 relationship.

Foundation. Briefly, this approach involves measuring the temperature differences, at a given site, between skin and clothing surface and between skin and air to obtain an efficiency factor (F_{cl}) for sensible (nonevaporative) heat loss. Then, knowing the convective and radiative heat transfer coefficients at the clothing surface, the effective clo value for that site may be calculated. The surface convection coefficient is determined at the site from the weight loss of a napthalene ball positioned near the clothing surface (Nishi and Gagge, 1970). Estimation of the evaporative characteristics of the clothing is less direct and requires measurement of physiological factors such as metabolic rate and respiratory losses. The humidity of the environment in which the subject is working is gradually raised until his skin is totally wet, as indicated by a distinct change in the rate of rise in body temperature. At this point, maximal evaporative cooling E_{max} and zero body heat storage are assumed to exist. From a total heat balance written for this critical environment, E_{max} may be calculated and an evaporative efficiency factor F_{pcl} derived, knowing the surface evaporative transfer coefficient h_e. At normal barometric pressure, this coefficient is 2.2 times the convective transfer coefficient h_e according to the "Modified Lewis Relation," as noted earlier.

Two other developments are worth mentioning in connection with this discussion of progress in evaluating body motion effects. The first is the use of a sensitive scale to follow a subject's weight loss during activity which, in the absence of dripping sweat, is equal to the water evaporated from the skin and clothing (plus respiratory loss). Nishi *et al.* (1975), in discussing their procedure, reported excellent agreement between E_{max} values derived from weight loss (*i.e.*, water evaporation rate times the latent heat of evaporation at skin temperature) and values derived from a total heat balance for the critical environment. From weight loss data during each "sweating" manikin study at USARIEM, we also find that the published latent heat values are applicable for deriving evaporative heat loss, provided the clothing ensemble consists of no more than two thin layers and does not become extremely wet; for heavier ensembles, however, the apparent latent heat (kcal of evaporative loss per kilogram of water loss) is lower than normal. Simply stated, water evaporated from the clothing is not 100% effective in removing heat from the skin, since some heat is obtained from the ambient air and clothing. Fortunately, apparent latent heat data are already available for a wide variety of clothing systems, allowing accurate estimates of evaporative dissipation regardless of the type of clothing worn.

The second development, use of a rapid-scan infrared camera (AGA Thermovision) to map clothing surface temperature, should simplify the measurement of Nishi's local F_{cl} values for nonevaporative heat transfer. Rather than employing thermocouples or other sensors to measure clothing temperature during activity, the subject could simply be stopped for the few seconds needed for the camera to make a complete thermal scan from a given direction. This brief halt in activity would not change the surface temperature pattern established during activity. An AGA thermogram would produce more information than could be used, since a skin temperature value is also required for calculating each local F_{cl} value; this is no shortcoming since the skin sites measured can be increased to any desired number. Of course, to calculate the insulating value at each site, one also requires a value for h_c (measured by napthalene sublimation), so that there is a practical limit to the number of local insulating values which could be determined. In addition, the h_c evaluations and thermal scan with the AGA require separate experiments since the napthalene balls would interfere with the scan.

Since the "pumping" coefficients associated with body motion can be more easily measured using a physical device, attempts are also being made to develop an electrically heated manikin with sufficient articulation and appropriate control mechanisms to allow duplication of human movement. Mecheels (1971) has described the walking manikin in use at the Hohenstein Institute, Germany, earlier in this book and elsewhere. A second manikin, which can simulate pedaling motions on a bicycle as well as stand erect, has been developed by Madsen and Fanger (1975), at the Technical University of Denmark. This manikin is also equipped with an internal water-fed system for "sweat" production. No results on studies with this manikin have yet been published.

REFERENCES

Belding, H. S., H. D. Russell, R. C. Darling and G. E. Folk. "Analysis of Factors Concerned in Maintaining Energy Balance for Dressed Men in Extreme Cold; Effects of Activity on the Protective Value and Comfort of an Arctic Uniform," *Am. J. Physiol.* 149:223 (1947).

Breckenridge, J. R. and R. F. Goldman. "Clothing, the Interface Between Man and His Environment: Resistance Against Meteorological Stimulus," in *Progress in Biometerology,* Vol. 1, Part 2, Chapter 7. Lisse, The Netherlands: Swets and Zeitlinger, 1976).

Breckenridge, J. R. and A. H. Woodcock. "Effects of Wind on Insulation of Arctic Clothing," Quartermaster Climatic Research Laboratory, Report No. 164, Lawrence, Mass. (1950).

Fonseca, G. F. and J. R. Breckenridge. "Wind Penetration Through Fabric Systems, Part I," *Text. Res. J.* 35:95-103 (1965a).

Fonseca, G. F. and J. R. Breckenridge. "Wind Penetration Through Fabric Systems, Part II," *Text. Res. J.* 35:221-227 (1965b).

Gagge, A. P., A. C. Burton and H. C. Bazett. "A Practical System of Units for the Description of the Heat Exchange of Man with His Environment," *Science* 94:428-430 (1941).

Givoni, B. and R. F. Goldman. "Predicting Rectal Temperature Response to Work, Environment and Clothing," *J. Appl. Physiol.* 32:812-821 (1972).

Goldman, R. F. "Systematic Evaluation of Thermal Aspects of Air Crew Protective Systems," in *Conference Proc. No. 25, Advisory Group for Aerospace Research and Development* (Paris: AGARD, 1967).

Goldman, R. F. and J. R. Breckenridge. "Etude des Effets Physiologiques du Vetement en Rapport Avec Ses Proprietes Biophysiques," *Cahiers de l'Association Francaisede Biometerologie* 3:33-36 (1970).

Haisman, M. F. and R. F. Goldman. "Physiological Evaluations of Armored Vests in Hot-Wet and Hot-Dry Climates," *Ergonomics* 17:1-12 (1974).

Madsen, T. L. and P. O. Fanger. Personal Communication (1975).

Mecheels, J. "Die Messung der Functionellen Wirkung der Kleidung Auf den Menschen," *Melliand Textilberichte* 52 (1971).

Nishi, Y. and A. P. Gagge. "Direct Evaluation of Convective Heat Transfer Coefficient by Napthalene Sublimation," *J. Appl. Physiol.* 29:830-838 (1970).

Nishi, Y. and A. P. Gagge. "Mathematical Model of Man's Heat Exchange with His Thermal Environment," *AICHE Symposium Series* 70:226-232 (1974).

Nishi, Y., R. R. Gonzales and A. P. Gagge. "Direct Measurement of Clothing Heat Transfer Properties During Sensible and Insensible Heat Exchange with Thermal Environment," ASHRAE, Paper No. 2371 (1975).

Woodcock, A. H. "Moisture Transfer in Textile Systems, Part I," *Text. Res. J.* 32:628-633 (1962).

Chapter 12

THE EFFECTS OF DESIGN AND DEGREE OF CLOSURE ON MICROCLIMATE AIR EXCHANGE IN LIGHTWEIGHT CLOTH COATS

J. L. Shivers

Department of Home Economics
Brescia College
University of Western Ontario
London, Ontario, Canada

K. Yeh, L. Fourt and S. M. Spivak

Department of Textiles and Consumer Economics
University of Maryland
College Park, Maryland 20742

INTRODUCTION

One primary function of clothing is to aid in maintaining physiological thermal balance. This refers to the proper relationship between body heat production and heat loss and may be controlled by modification of the microclimate air between clothing and skin. Stationary microclimate air provides insulation from a cold environment. Under work or exercise conditions or in warm environments, however, it is desirable to have limited and controlled exchange of microclimate air with ambient air (outside the clothing assembly) in order to dissipate excess body heat and moisture and thereby maintain thermal balance. According to Crockford and co-workers (1972), factors which influence the rate of microclimate air exchange are clothing permeability, wind speed, body movements, clothing design and fabric properties.

Crockford *et al.* (1972) interpreted the exchange of microclimate air as an exponential process, and derived rates of mixing of the microclimate with external air using a nitrogen trace gas technique. They assumed the exchange

rate between the microclimate and ambient air to be a first-order reaction of
the form:

$$\frac{dP}{dt} = k (P_O - P) \tag{1}$$

where P = oxygen concentration at time t

               P_O = eventual concentration of oxygen in the system (0.21)

               k = rate constant.

This states that the rate of return of ambient air to the microclimate (*i.e.*, rate
of increase of oxygen concentration) is proportional to the difference between
the oxygen concentrations in the microclimate and in ambient air.

Hollies, Fourt *et al.* (1973) used the same assumption of an exponential
process but limited their analysis to obtaining the half-time, $t^{1/2}$, *i.e.,* time
for one-half the accomplishment of mixing, as shown below:

$$t^{1/2} = \frac{\ln 2}{k} \tag{2}$$

where k = rate constant as in Equation 1. Assuming a first-order reaction, the
half-time would be independent of both initial concentration and also volume.
The half-time can be readily obtained from experimental data. One should
keep in mind that large half-times go with slow rates of mixing; and shorter
half-times with more rapid rates of mixing. This paper limits its discussion
to half-times.

Crockford and Rosenblum (1974) recently reported a method for estimating total microclimate volume by enclosing garment and wearer in an air
tight plastic suit, extracting the air and then measuring the volume of air required to reinflate the microclimate.

Most of the research related to microclimate air exchange has been directed
toward men's specialized clothing assemblies made of treated nonpermeable
fabrics for use in extreme climates by the military or industrial sectors. Conventional clothing made of permeable fabrics has not been investigated except
for the pilot study by Crockford *et al.* (1972) which applied the nitrogen
trace-gas technique to quantifying air exchange rates in clothing made of
permeable fabrics. According to Fourt and Hollies (1970), "very little is
known regarding the interactions of clothing design, body motion and internal ventilation." Since there are few reports of studies on the relationship
between garment design and efficiency of microclimate flux, the need for
such an investigation is obvious.

The present chapter therefore deals with preliminary studies to explore
air exchange between ambient air and the clothing–skin microclimate in
lightweight cloth coats; to assess the influence of differences in garment design

features and mode of use; and lastly to examine the suitability of the nitrogen trace-gas technique and associated methods of data analysis in measuring microclimate air exchange under the above conditions. The coats prepared for this study are similar to commercially available garments made of permeable inner and outer fabrics. The main variable is sleeve design; other variables are degree of closure at neck and waist, position at which air exchange is measured (front, back or arm microclimate) and subject movement.

EXPERIMENTAL PROCEDURE

Variable Sleeve Coat Designs

A basic design for a ladies lightweight cloth coat with center front zipper opening and convertible collar was developed. Two variations of the basic style, each with a different type of sleeve, were designed. One coat was made with a set-in sleeve and the other with a low-dolman sleeve to achieve a range of closeness of fit through the sleeve types, keeping all other dimensions exactly alike.

Both coats were identical in fabric, color, trim and dimensions except for the upper sleeve. The armhole circumferences varied from 46.7 cm (18-3/8 in.) for the set-in sleeve to 66.5 cm (26-3/16 in.) for the low-dolman sleeve, a range of 19.8 cm (7-13/16 in.). The armhole circumference measurement was made following the natural seamline in the set-in sleeve coat; for the low-dolman style, the measurement was made over the shoulder in the natural seamline position down to the low point of the respective seamlines in front and back and following the seamline under the arm.

The outer fabric was red polyester/cotton poplin of 220 g/m^2 (6.6 oz/yd^2). White, 100% acetate taffeta of 81 g/m^2 (2.4 oz/yd^2) was used for all the linings. A hair canvas of 60% cotton, 30% rayon and 10% goat hair was used to interface the collars.

Sleeve linings were set in by hand and attached to the outer sleeve in order to keep inner and outer fabrics together in the armhole area. It was felt that this method would facilitate more accurate measures of air mixing.

Selection of the Sample

Two female subjects participated in the study. It was necessary that both participants be of the same size to fit the coats in a like manner. Accordingly, both subjects were very similar in physical measurements such as height, weight, chest, waist and hips.

Method for Measuring Half-Times for
Microclimate Air Exchange

The nitrogen trace-gas method developed by Crockford, Crowder and Prestidge (1972) as modified by Hollies, Fourt *et al.* (1973) was used. Figure 1 shows a schematic illustration of the experimental setup. One end of a

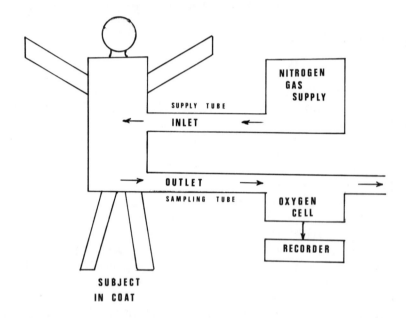

Figure 1. Schematic illustration of the experimental setup.

(0.8-cm or 5/16-in. diameter) polyvinyl chloride *supply* tube was connected to a tank of compressed nitrogen gas. The other end of the supply tube was closed at its extremity, but had a number of small diamond shaped holes randomly distributed over the last 20 cm (8 in.) from the closed end. This perforated portion of the tube was sewn to a strip of nylon ribbon which was safety-pinned inside the coat at marked locations.

One end of a 0.3-cm (1/8-in.) diameter polyvinyl chloride *sampling* tube was connected to an oxygen cell (Bacharach Instrument Co.). The other end of the sampling tube was also sewn to nylon ribbon and safety-pinned inside the coat at marked locations. A vacuum pump was used to draw the microclimate air mixture through the sampling tube and through the oxygen cell at approximately 0.85–0.99 m^3/hr (30–35 ft^3/hr). The emf output from the oxygen cell was fed to a strip chart recorder.

The oxygen cell and recorder were calibrated each day against both 100% nitrogen and the oxygen content in room air. To prepare for testing, compressed nitrogen at 140 kPa (20 lb/in.^{2}) pressure was fed through the supply tube into the airspace inside the coat until the microclimate nitrogen concentration reached saturation. The nitrogen supply was halted, and testing simultaneously was begun measuring the time in seconds for return of the microclimate oxygen content to a point halfway between the starting concentration and the ambient concentration. This halfway point was used as the measure of microclimate/ambient air exchange, and defined as "half-time, sec." Figure 2 illustrates a representative curve of the type obtained during these experiments.

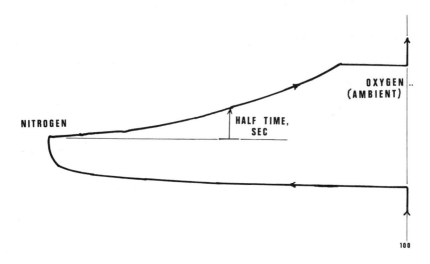

Figure 2. A representative "row data" curve.

Between each individual test, the subject unzipped the coat, pulled it off the shoulders and flapped it to flush out all traces of nitrogen before the next test. The absence of nitrogen excess was confirmed by allowing the recorder to register 100% normal room air before proceeding.

The coats were completely zipped on all tests when nitrogen was fed into the microclimate. At this point, for the tests done in a rest position, the subject stood absolutely still with arms relaxed until signaled at the end of the test. For the tests made with an open neckline, the subject was told to "unzip" and exactly as that was being done, the nitrogen was shut off. The same procedure was used for the tests done on open neck coats during exercise. Before the nitrogen was introduced the subject turned in the direction she would walk. When signaled, the nitrogen was shut off as the subject unzipped the coat to a marked point and started walking four steps forward and backward, swinging the arms to the beat of a metronome set at 112 beats per min.

In order to standardize the tightness of the belt for the belted coat tests, a 2.5-cm (1-in.) tuck was pinched out at the back before the belt was tied, and then released before the nitrogen was turned on.

The complete set of tests was replicated both on each subject and on different days, providing a mean of four data points for each experiment. One individual test required an average of about 2 min, including the time needed to flush the microclimate of all traces of nitrogen from the previous test, readjusting the coat, filling it with nitrogen and allowing air exchange to occur until the recorder indicated about 80% normal microclimate air.

Position of Supply and Sampling Tubes

The supply and sampling tubes were each secured in a preselected position in either the back, sleeve or front of each coat, as noted below.

Back of Coat

The supply tube entered through the right sleeve. The perforated end was centered and pinned across the back, with the tube 8.9 cm (3-1/2 in.) below the neckline at center back. The sampling tube entered from the lower edge of the coat with the open end placed 17.8 cm (7 in.) below the neckline at center back.

Left Sleeve

The supply tube was positioned on the inner sleeve back, 2.5 cm (1 in.) from the lengthwise seam. The center of the 20 cm (8 in.) perforated tube end was placed 40.6 cm (16 in.) from the bottom of the sleeve. Total sleeve length was 46.4 cm (18-1/4 in.)

Front of Coat

The supply tube entered through the right sleeve across the front and down, 2.5 cm (1 in.) from the zipper coil and parallel to it. The sampling tube entered through the left sleeve across the front and was pinned 2.5 cm (1 in.) from the zipper coil 20 cm (8 in.) below the center front neckline.

RESULTS

Data Analysis on Ventilation Half-Times

The data were grouped into three sets of interactions between the main variable, sleeve design, and the secondary variables: position of microclimate sample, degree of closure at waist and neckline and subject movement. Each set consisted of the data at rest and the data for exercise. Half-times for air mixing in the set-in and low-dolman sleeve styles are reported below.

An analysis of variance for factorial design (Dixon, 1971) was used for statistical analysis. This method identified single variables or combinations of variables within each set of data which significantly contributed to differences in half-time ventilation.

The mean points and ranges for each significant variable or combination of variables were also plotted on a graph to identify the conditions which contributed to most efficient air exchange.

Set I tested the effects between extremes of sleeve design (set-in and low-dolman) and extremes of closure (open neckline/unbelted; closed neckline/fully belted) in all sampling positions (back, arm and front microclimates).

The statistical analysis of the data for Set I are summarized in Table I.

Table I. Analysis of Variance for Ventilation Half-Times, Extremes of Closure and Sleeve Design, All Sampling Positions (Microclimates)
Set I

Source of Variation	Degrees of Freedom	Mean Square	F Ratio
Rest			
Sleeve design	1	27.60	1.46
Position	2	216.20	11.50 [a]
Degree of closure	1	106.80	5.78 [b]
Sleeve design/position	2	29.71	1.58
Sleeve design/degree of closure	1	10.83	0.57
Position/degree of closure	2	270.86	14.41 [a]
Sleeve design/position/degree of closure	2	2.73	0.14
Within replicates	36	18.81	
Exercise			
Sleeve design	1	0.11	0.04
Position	2	32.01	11.68 [a]
Degree of closure	1	1.51	0.55
Sleeve design/position	2	0.76	0.28
Sleeve design/degree of closure	1	0.20.	0.07
Position/degree of closure	2	15.87	5.79 [a]
Sleeve design/position/degree of closure	2	0.88	0.32
Within replicates	36	2.74	

[a] significant at 0.01 level   [b] significant at 0.05 level

These data indicate that when the subject is standing at ease, the combination of position of the microclimate sample and degree of closure contribute most to variation in half-times for air mixing. Each of these variables significantly affects the ventilation half-time, the position of sampling to a more significant extent than degree of closure by itself.

When the subject is walking, thus creating a bellows effect within the coat, the position of the microclimate sample contributes most to variability. Variation of half-times as a result of the combination of position and degree of closure is also significant at the $p \leqslant 0.01$ level.

Figures 3 and 4 illustrate some of the above relationships. Figure 3 is a graph of the mean ventilation half-times at each microclimate for rest and exercise. The half-times for rest are all longer and more heterogeneous than those for exercise. This result was expected because bellows action contributes to more rapid air exchange. Range of half-times due to bellows action is reduced by the exercise, and the absolute value of the half-time is smaller for the exercise. All half-times crowd together as they become shorter.

Figure 3 also illustrates that air mixing occurs most rapidly in the arm microclimate for rest and exercise and takes the longest time in the back microclimate for rest and exercise.

Figure 4 illustrates the effect of combinations of position of microclimate sample and degree of closure on ventilation half-times. There is greater range in half-times for rest than for exercise. The most rapid air mixing is in the

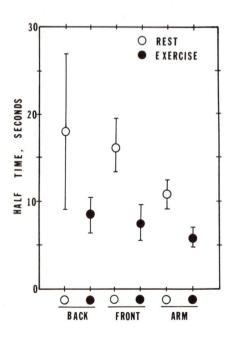

Figure 3. Mean ventilation half-times for each microclimate – Set I.

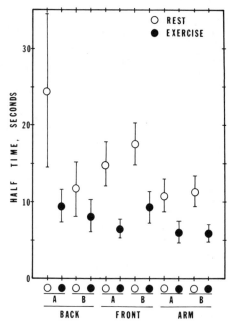

Figure 4. Mean ventilation half-times for each microclimate and degree of closure – Set I.

arm microclimate, and degree of closure has no significant effect on the half-time in this location. In the front, the open neck, unbelted condition promotes more rapid mixing than the closed neckline, belted condition. In the back, the results are reversed: the closed neckline, belted condition greatly reduces the half-time for air mixing.

Set II tested the effects of the closure variables (open neckline, closed neckline, belted, unbelted) in the two extremes of sleeve design on the half-time for air mixing in the *back* microclimate.

The statistical analysis of the data for Set II are summarized in Table II. Results indicate that when the subject is standing at ease, there is a significant relationship between the coat worn belted or unbelted and ventilation half-times in the back. There were no significant relationships between any of the variables (separately or in combination) for the tests done with the subject walking.

Figure 5 illustrates some of these effects. It may be seen that the ventilation half-time in the back is greatly reduced when the coat is worn belted as compared to half-times when the coat is worn unbelted. This difference was statistically significant only for the tests done with the subject standing at rest.

Table II. Analysis of Variance for Ventilation Half-Times, Closure Variables on Back Microclimate
Set II

Source of Variation	Degrees of Freedom	Mean Square	F Ratio
Rest			
Neck closure	1	1.32	0.03
Belt or unbelt	1	1150.80	25.09 a
Sleeve design	1	112.13	2.45
Neck closure/belt or unbelt	1	1.40	0.03
Neck closure/sleeve design	1	1.09	0.02
Belt or unbelt/sleeve design	1	39.38	0.86
Neck closure/belt or unbelt/sleeve design	1	5.20	0.11
Within replicates	24	45.86	
Exercise			
Neck closure	1	0.41	0.11
Belt or unbelt	1	8.82	2.34
Sleeve design	1	1.81	0.48
Neck closure/belt or unbelt	1	0.85	0.23
Neck closure/sleeve design	1	0.32	0.08
Belt or unbelt/sleeve design	1	0.25	0.07
Neck closure/belt or unbelt/sleeve design	1	0.08	0.02
Within replicates	24	3.77	

a significant at 0.01 level

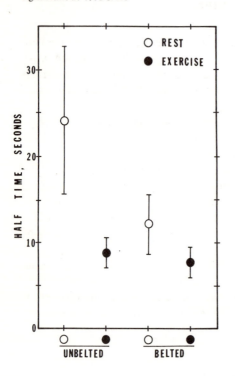

Figure 5. Mean ventilation half-times for the back microclimate, belted and unbelted — Set II.

Set III tested the effects of the closure variables (open neckline, closed neckline, belted, unbelted) in the two extremes of sleeve design on the half-time for air mixing in the *arm* microclimate. The statistical analysis of the Set III data are summarized in Table III. These data indicate no significant relationships between any of the variables (separately or in combination) and ventilation half-times measured in the arm microclimate.

Table III. Analysis of Variance for Ventilation Half-Times, Closure Variables on Arm Microclimate Set III

Source of Variation	Degrees of Freedom	Mean Square	F Ratio
Rest			
Neck closure	1	2.10	0.70
Belt or unbelt	1	0.10	0.03
Sleeve design	1	0.55	0.18
Neck closure/belt or unbelt	1	0.91	0.30
Neck closure/sleeve design	1	0.45	0.12
Belt or unbelt/sleeve design	1	2.31	0.76
Neck closure/belt or unbelt/sleeve design	1	1.71	0.57
Within replicates	24	3.02	
Exercise			
Neck closure	1	0.32	0.22
Belt or unbelt	1	1.53	1.09
Sleeve design	1	0.10	0.07
Neck closure/belt or unbelt	1	0.66	0.47
Neck closure/sleeve design	1	0.28	0.20
Belt or unbelt/sleeve design	1	0.41	0.29
Neck closure/belt or unbelt/sleeve design	1	1.13	0.80
Within replicates	24	1.41	

Figure 6 illustrates that air mixing is more rapid and less variable in the arm than in the back (Figure 5). Half-times are very similar for the tests done with the subject standing at rest and for the tests done with the subject walking, regardless of whether the coats are worn belted or unbelted.

Physical Tests on the Fabric Used

Fabric stiffness and porosity are known to contribute to microclimate-ambient air exchange in clothing (Hollies *et al.*, 1973). Therefore, measures of these properties were conducted on the outer and lining fabric and are reported as flexural rigidity and air permeability in Tables IV and V, respectively.

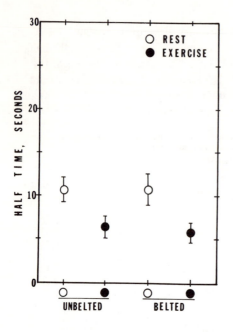

Figure 6. Mean ventilation half-times for the arm microclimate; belted and unbelted — Set III.

Table IV. Measures of Flexural Rigidity

Fabric Tested	Bending Length, c (cm)	Weight per Unit Area, w (g/cm^2) (x 10^{-3})	Flexural Rigidity G = wc^3 (g-cm)	Overall Fabric Flexural Rigidity[a] $G_O = \sqrt{G_w \times G_f}$ (g-cm)
Poplin		22.0		3.7
Warp	6.3		5.5	
Filling	4.8		2.4	
Taffeta		8.0		1.2
Warp	5.5		1.3	
Filling	5.1		1.7	

[a] (Peirce, 1930).

Table V. Measures of Air Permeability

Fabric Tested	Air Permeability m^3/m^2 - S (ft^3/ft^2 - min) @ 124 pascals (0.5 in.) Water Pressure	
Poplin only	0.069	(13.5)
Taffeta only	0.080	(15.7)
Poplin on top of Taffeta	0.037	(7.3)
Taffeta on top of Poplin	0.038	(7.5)

DISCUSSION

For the materials used, it would appear that the fabrics (especially the poplin) had a high measure of flexural rigidity and together had a low level of air permeability. A high degree of fabric flexural rigidity contributes to the fabric standing away from the body, thus maximizing microclimate volume and air exchange for each sleeve design. Fourt and Harris have compared the air permeability of several fabrics and report a range of from 0.005 m^3/sm^2 (0.9 ft^3/ft^2-min) for a wind-resistant cloth to 6.6 m^3/sm^2 (1300 ft^3/ft^2-min) for mosquito netting (Newburgh, 1968). The comparatively low air permeability of the fabrics employed in the current study would further contribute to testing the influence of sleeve design, as most air movement would be expected to occur through garment openings rather than through the fabrics.

Position of microclimate sample contributed most significantly to the variance of half-time ventilation. The logic behind this result should be clear: the microclimate volume in the back of an unbelted coat is greater than the volume in the front at chest level or in the upper arm. The coat is well fitted to the shoulders and arms in a natural, relaxed position, and tends to separate inner arm volume from front and back. Therefore, each of these areas is relatively sealed off from the others.

Crockford et al. (1972) have stated that microclimate volume will affect the rate of mixing. If the rate of introduction of new air is constant, the larger the volume, the longer the time for mixing, but if the larger volume increases the rate of admission of new air, this will shorten the time for mixing. However, a method for quantifying microclimate volume has only recently been reported (Crockford and Rosenblum, 1974). If this method for whole garments could be adapted and related to the current investigation, the results might well be different. It was expected that increased microclimate volume in the upper arm area would significantly contribute to efficient air mixing. The fact that no difference in half-times for air mixing between sleeve designs was shown may be explained. When the arm is lowered to a natural position, the additional inner space created by the low-dolman sleeve is modified by the fabric folding over itself under the arm. The resulting microclimate volume is probably very similar to that created by the set-in sleeve, although the widest sleeve coat has a looser fit and was, therefore, subjectively judged most comfortable.

The individual data points for measurements taken in the back microclimate of the unbelted coats were quite heterogeneous, but overall averages demonstrate a significantly longer time necessary for air mixing than in the arm and front. Through observation of the tent-shaped coats as they were worn, it was apparent that the back inner volume is greater than the front inner volume which in turn is greater than inner arm volume. Of the three volumes, the back is subject to the greatest fluctuation due to the coat hanging from the shoulders. Posture, which may be very erect at the beginning of a set of tests, but may change as the time passes, will obviously affect the amount of inner space. Also, the amount of microclimate volume will vary between subjects of equal weight as a result of different distribution of body weight, although the body measurements of the two subjects in this experiment were very similar.

Measures of air exchange taken in the front were subject to different influences. The front of the coat forms a natural seal across the shoulders and again across the chest, thus reducing the inner volume and also reducing the fluctuation of inner volume. The closed neckline/belted and open neckline/unbelted conditions had opposite effects on rates of air mixing in the front and back, and had no significant effect in the arm position.

The open neckline, unbelted coat increased back volume (because of being unrestricted at the waist) relative to the closed neckline, belted condition. However, the open neckline and unbelting did not produce more efficient air mixing in the back. Air exchange in the back was most efficient when the coat was belted. This is apparently due to a volume effect, in which reduced back volume due to belting contributed to shorter half-times. Alternately, the open neckline, unbelted condition did contribute to more efficient air exchange in the front position, which would appear to be isolated from the back. Apparently, the chimney effect is operative in the front position, but not in the back or arm position.

The effect of exercise consistently reduced half-times and made them more homogeneous in both sleeve designs, all positions of microclimate sample, and under all conditions of closure, although the effect of exercise was very limited in the arm microclimate. The reduced and similar half-times as a result of exercise may be explained by the concept of forced ventilation through bellows action, promoting air exchange through the openings in the garment. The differences in sleeve design were not significant in influencing microclimate air exchange.

The method as used does not include the concept of microclimate volume which appears strongly related to the half-times of mixing when coats are worn belted or unbelted. Where volume differences do occur, further thought may be needed before this can be interpreted as being directly related to more or less efficient air mixing. For such situations, a rate of mixing may be a more accurate and discriminating measure of air exchange. Further, the current method to objectively quantify comfort in terms of ventilation half-times does not detect subjective differences between styles and fit which are readily perceived when the coats are worn. These may be judged as shortcomings of the trace-gas technique or of the way it was used for this study.

CONCLUSION

Bellows ventilation induced through exercise was found to reduce half-times under all conditions. There were, however, no significant differences in ventilation half-times between sleeve designs. Significant differences between open and closed neckline, and between extremes of garment closure, were found in the front position of microclimate only. This front "chimney effect" was not observed in other positions.

The data further imply that ventilation half-times may be influenced by microclimate volume; the greater the volume, the longer the time necessary for air exchange, and vice versa. This suggests that for sizeable volume differences, the assumption of a first-order reaction rate may not be completely valid and volume effects may have to be considered. This might include quantifying microclimate volume in garment subassemblies.

The present investigations also support the concept that specific microclimate volumes within the garments are not necessarily continuous but indeed may be separate and isolated entities.

ACKNOWLEDGMENTS

The authors thank Londontown Manufacturing Company of Baltimore, Maryland for providing the outer fabric used for the coats.

REFERENCES

Crockford, G. W., M. Crowder and S. P. Prestidge. "A Trace-Gas Technique for Measuring Clothing Microclimate Air Exchange Rates," *Brit. J. Ind. Med.* 29:378-386 (1972).

Crockford, G. W. and H. A. Rosenblum. "The Measurement of Clothing Microclimate Volumes," *Clothing Res. J.* 2:109-114 (1974).

Dixon, W. J., Ed. *Biomedical Computer Programs* (Berkeley: University of California Press, 1971), pp. 495-510.

Fourt, L. and N. R. S. Hollies. *Clothing: Comfort and Function* (New York: Marcel Dekker, 1970), p. 43.

Hollies, N. R. S., L. Fourt, G. Arnold and N. Custer. "Use Type Tests for Comfort and Effectiveness of Firemen's Turnout Coats," U. S. Department of Commerce, Contract No. NBS 2-35929, COM-74-11075/OGI (1973), pp. 18-26.

Newburgh, L. H. Ed. *Physiology of Heat Regulation and the Science of Clothing* (New York: Hafner, 1968), p. 308.

Peirce, F. T. "The Handle of Cloth as a Measurable Quantity," *J. Text. Inst.* 21:T377-T416 (1930).